The Fanatic Resolve

Extreme Mission Devotional & Journal

Janell R. Ward

Project Editors: Diane Owen, Kathy Slone, Nancy Ward

Cover Design by: Lyn Rayn

Internal Design Assistant: Sam Justice

Due to the NIV translation not capitalizing the pronouns "he" and "him" when speaking of God, this book has followed Biblical formatting.

Printed in the United States of America.

Dedication

Dedicated to every past, present, and future fanatic who has refused the food of spiritual mediocrity.

Dedicated to those who have lived and died for the one they have not seen.

And dedicated to those who understand what it means to be found standing.

Table of Contents

Preface

What if we were crazy about God? What if we were radically enthused to carry his cause on the shoulders of our existence? How powerful it would be if we maintained uncompromising hunger for his truth, love, and righteousness, and then yielded ourselves to make it evident in our lives! Matthew 11:12 says, *"From the days of John the Baptist until now, the kingdom of heaven has been forcefully advancing, and forceful men lay hold of it."*

Laying hold of heaven's kingdom is about grasping the whole spectrum of who Christ is in us. Maintaining and living out passionate desire for the Lord is what being given to the fanatic resolve means. Fanaticism is about the zeal, enthusiasm, and craze that come with being madly in love with Jesus Christ. Sir Winston Churchill said, "A fanatic is one who can't change his mind and won't change the subject." How amazing it would be to become a people who refused to change our minds about being wholly in love with the Lord! How awesome it would be to keep Christ as the subject of each moment, where all things pointed to him and his power to restore, heal, and save. However, there is no benefit of having desire without devotion. What profit is passion with no action? What good is the glory of the proclamation if we don't submit to the vocation?

The decision, determination, and dedication are the colors that create the resolve. The resolve is about standing unmovable in a faithless, hopeless, and loveless world—you resolve to understand God and the supremacy of his life; just like Paul declared: *"I want to know Christ and the power of his resurrection and the fellowship of sharing in his sufferings, becoming like him in his death,"* (Philippians 3:10). You resolve your heart to obey his decrees, your mind to let him have control, and your soul to fall into his grace. Then once you've clutched him with your heart, soul, and mind, you will find yourself fulfilling the *"most important"* commandment: Mark 12:29-30 *"The most important one," answered Jesus, "is this: '...Love the Lord your God with all your heart and with all your soul and with all your mind and with all your strength.*

Once one is fanatically resolved to unite their life with God's, they will be left with a radical enthusiasm for the spreading of the gospel message. 1 John 2:6 says, *"Whoever claims to live in him must live as Jesus did."* In order to *"live as Jesus did"*, we must be willing to yield ourselves to obtaining his unrelenting heart for people! Jesus didn't compromise our souls for his comfort. No, he was fanatically resolved to bring us close.

God's radical love demands a radical response, and our response should be no less purposeful and passionate than that of Isaiah, when he said, *"... 'Here am I. Send me!'"*(Isaiah 6:8). Remember that you can lay hold of the things that Christ has for you because you have been sought and saved by his beautiful sacrifice. Seize, bolt, run, and chase the heart of God. And in your chasing of him, you will become like him, and *"...you will receive power when the Holy Spirit comes on you; and you will be... (his)... witnesses in Jerusalem, and in all Judea and Samaria, and to the ends of the earth.'"* (Acts 1:8).

How this book works:
- For 2 week missions: If you are venturing on a 2 week mission project, begin reading this book 7 days before your trip. Based on when you return home, you will also have a 7-10 day follow up on vital concepts about continuing in what you've learned. Use the provided space to write about what God is doing in you. If you need more space to write, flip to the back where there are extra pages to journal. Be stretched and blessed on your journey!
- For 4 week missions: Start 4 days before you leave. Read through and think about each lesson carefully. Allow the Lord to mold and shape your heart for the next month of your life! The last 7 days will serve to prepare you for your return home; starting the next season of your life with a revived heart and mind is vital for maintenance of your spiritual growth. Use the provided space to write about what God is doing in you. If you need more space to write, flip to the back where there are extra pages to journal. Enjoy your journey! And keep your eyes on Jesus!
- For 6-8 week missions: Go through at your own pace. Make sure, if possible, to read through the first 3 days before you venture off. Since you will be on the field for more mission days than there are devotional days, you can look to the themes of each day and choose whatever lesson you feel your heart needs to hear. Use all the space

you can to also write notes about new things God is showing you and how he is faithfully working on the field. Make sure to take your daily time with the Lord; it's vital for productive ministry and staying rooted (John 15:4).

- <u>The Mission's Challenge:</u> If you are longing to be more active in sharing your faith at home, pick a start date. Make sure to remain open to sharing the gospel everywhere you are. The activities will stretch you and help you to step out in your faith. Have fun creating a new atmosphere of evangelism in your city!

Dear Warrior,
I pray that you will be rooted and established in love and that the whole world will wonder who God is on account of your life. I pray you will boldly and fervently resolve to reveal the glory of the Lord, and that as you exude flames of faith you will set the world on fire.

Day 1

Fellowship of Fire

Theme: Embracing the Call

The people living in darkness have seen a great light; on those living in the land of the shadow of death a light has dawned."

Matthew 4:16

How wonderful it is that you were called by name, that the Commander of love sought you out, and that he summoned you to journey with him (Isaiah 49:1, Luke 19:10, Matthew 4:19). Maybe you don't fully understand the reason God would request you to mission with him in streets, slums, and villages, or why he would want you to converse with people you've never met. Perhaps you aren't fully confident about passionately proclaiming his message to close friends, co-workers, and people at home. Even if you've been on missions several times and are well practiced at evangelizing, questions creep up such as, "How can *I* preach the news of Christ? How can *I* walk like him when my ways are blemished and my strength is little?" It's easy to feel unqualified, unready, and undeserving of doing the work of the Lord. Just like you, the Apostle Paul knew that he was unable to carry the task of being Jesus to the world in his human efforts. He knew that without the power of the Lord he would be unable to do anything. But the Lord said to Paul, "*'My grace is sufficient for you, for my power is made perfect in weakness'*" (2 Corinthians 12:9).

Many other disciples felt unqualified to live a life like Jesus as well. Most of them didn't even consider themselves worthy to *die* as Jesus had died— hence, the reason for Peter being crucified on an X-shaped cross, upside down.[1] The disciples were fanatics for the cause of the Lord. The Bible never says the disciples were perfect; it says they were *passionate* (Matthew 26:35). It doesn't say they were flawless; it says they were *fervent* (Matthew 12:49-50). It doesn't say they were optimal; it says they were *obedient* (Matthew 4:20).

Sometimes it's easy to wonder what good can come from being obedient because it doesn't always seem to be appealing or profitable. We forget that it was through the obedience of Christ that the entire world was given the ability to attain freedom. So the question is, "What will prolong our mindset of evangelism?" or "How do we not only jumpstart our zeal, but how do we remain obedient?" All we need to do is look at what sustained Jesus. What was it that made him stay on the cross and not back down? The answer is *us*. Christ's ambition to save us poured from his acknowledgement of our human condition without him. *"We all, like sheep, have gone astray..."* (Isaiah 53:6). Jesus knew that without him humanity would subsist in a devastating, spiritual dilemma. The *only* action that ushers in freedom is obedience. Jesus knew that! It fueled his unrelenting decision to do whatever it took to bring us life, even if it was death (Philippians 2:8).

Yet, the question remains, what made his ambition fully and consistently transit into submission? The answer is that he had his eyes on the *promise*. Jesus fixated his heart on the vision which God wanted to make a reality. The vision is about setting people free: *"'I, the LORD, have called you in righteousness; I will take hold of your hand. I will keep you and will make you to be a covenant for the people and a light for the Gentiles, to open eyes that are blind, to free captives from prison and to release from the dungeon those who sit in darkness"* (Isaiah 42:6-7).

You catch the vision of people's lives without Jesus, and not only without Jesus but without *you*. You are a vital part of God's work on earth! Just as Christ's enthusiasm was birthed from your condition without him, so your fanatic fervor can be pumped up when you realize this about those who are lost: *"How, then, can they call on the one they have not believed in? And how can they believe in the one of whom they have not heard? And how can they hear without someone preaching to them?"* (Romans 10:14). Verse 15 goes on to say, *"And how can anyone preach unless they are sent? ..."* No one would ever hear the news of Christ if it weren't for you! You are his hands and feet on earth! Jesus left you with the commission to reach the globe. He said, *"Therefore go and make disciples of all nations, baptizing them in the name of the Father and of the Son and of the Holy Spirit, and teaching them to obey everything I have commanded you. And surely I am with you always, to the very end of the age"* (Matthew 28:19-20).

"Here is a trustworthy saying: If we died with him, we will also live with him;" (2 Timothy 2:11). Gloriously, Christ calls you to take part in his submissive death (Matthew 16:24). However your death in Christ is not only what ushers in freedom; it's more so that you are resuscitated into *life* with Christ! Paul said, *"'I want to know Christ—yes, to know the power of his resurrection and participation in his sufferings, becoming like him in his death, and so, somehow, attaining to the resurrection from the dead..."* *(Philippians 3:10-11).* After Jesus rose from the dead, he met two men on the side of the road, and *"They asked each other, 'Were not our hearts burning within us while he talked with us on the road and opened the Scriptures to us?'"* (Luke 24:32). Likewise, once you have died in obedience for Christ and have been resurrected, your presence in other people's lives will have a burning impact.

Luke 4:17-19 says, *"The Spirit of the Lord is on me, because he has anointed me to proclaim good news to the poor. He has sent me to proclaim freedom for the prisoners and recovery of sight for the blind, to set the oppressed free, to proclaim the year of the Lord's favor.'"* Yes, the Spirit of the Lord is upon you, and the promise remains: *"... where the Spirit of the Lord is, there is freedom"* (2 Corinthians 3:17). Christ brought his Spirit here—right where you are, right inside of you, so that you, together with him, can create freedom for those who are bound! But it's *your* duty to seize the participation, to cling to the fellowship with the Lord. You must *choose* the fire of ambition and submission to God.

Jesus has faith in your abilities to go and reach people for him. He said that you could do even more things than he did: *"Very truly I tell you, whoever believes in me will do the works I have been doing, and they will do even greater things than these, because I am going to the Father"* (John 14:12). You will bring the blaze of freedom when you join the fellowship of Jesus Christ. Oh, what fire obedience brings— a holy fire that burns spiritual chains off people's lives! That is what the vision and the commission is about—the participation of the fellowship of fire burning up the sin and illuminating the prison of darkness. It's the promise. Freedom for the captives—it is the goal.

Remember that even if you don't fully understand why God is drawing you to evangelize, just be obedient. I charge you to never look at your life and see merely one person. Through the obedience of one person, the spiritual realm of people's lives was liberated (Romans 5:19)! How much more could you, walking as Christ, escort freedom into the lives of those around you? Yes, you are one person. Yes, you can impact your generation and generations to come. You can join the fellowship of fire through obedience and ignite flames of freedom all throughout the world!

Application:

Maybe you are ready to embrace the commission to evangelize and make disciples. Ambition is a great step! It's evidence that you are truly catching the vision. However, while ambition is wonderful, without the submission it is fleeting.

Take some time today to ask God what he wants to speak to you about before you venture off to be a witness. Remember that God makes all things new (2 Corinthians 5:17). Maybe you need him to make new your passion to reach people, or make new your resolve to actually do the things in your heart. Whatever it is, offer your clay hands and feet to God; he will mold them. Remember also that when you invited God into your life you married his *whole self.* Therefore, you also married his heart for missions.

Think about and answer these questions. If you need more journaling space there is ample room in the back of the book.

How does it make you feel to know that your life in Christ is a part of God's plan to rescue people from darkness?

_____

_____

_____

_____

_____

_____

_____

What are you looking forward to most about answering the call to preach the gospel?

_____

_____

_____

_____

_____

_____

_____

_____

Are you struggling with any hesitations about your call to evangelize? What are they?

_____

_____

_____

_____

_____

_____

_____

_____

_____

_____

_____

_____

_____

_____

_____

When was the last time you remember talking to someone about the Lord's work in your life? How did that experience mold your mindset about evangelizing now?

_____

_____

_____

_____

_____

_____

_____

_____

Remember that Christ said you could do even more than he did. Does it make you feel more passionate that you are administering freedom to captives or that God is walking with you while you do it? Which one, and why?

_____

_____

_____

_____

_____

_____

_____

_____

_____

_____

In one word, state what it is that you want God to be for you while you go out to minister. What one attribute do you need for him to fulfill for you while you kick-start your new life of evangelism? _____

In closing, be reassured that your obedience will ultimately change the lives of others for the better .Your acknowledgment of the vision and the commission will birth the submission and the ambition you need. What more does God want than willing and ready vessels? Allowing yourself to be conformed into the likeness of Christ and spreading of the gospel will cause a holy transition in the lives of others—that transition is freedom.

Verse to Remember: *For this is what the Lord has commanded us: "'I have made you a light for the Gentiles, that you may bring salvation to the ends of the earth'"* (Acts 13:47).

Quote to Consider: We must be global Christians with a global vision because our God is a global God. - John Stott[2]

Now, I implore you as a soldier of Jesus Christ, fight *the good fight…finish the race…*keep *the faith* (2 Timothy 4:7).

Day 2

Compassion Fashion

Theme: Obtaining God's Heart for the Lost

"This is what the LORD Almighty said: 'Administer true justice; show mercy and compassion to one another.

Zechariah 7:9

The year was around 1600 AD. Dutch painters emerged from cities such as Amsterdam, Haarlem, Dordrecht, and Delft. Innovation was stirring in their world of art; painters were becoming enamored with *reality*. From religious scenes to countryside landscapes, every feature of life was expressed through paint. But these Dutch painters weren't merely painting for enjoyment. They had a cause—they wanted people to see life as it actually was, to see the knowledge in Scriptures, and to be commonsensical in their everyday lives.[1]

Realism is wonderful. While reality for the Dutch artists was fields, churches, and ordinary life, reality for this generation is the latest fashions, rising stars, and new technologies. Because the world is visible, the eyes of humanity effortlessly become locked on external elements. However, there is another type of reality that is sometimes hard to see—the reality of the spiritual realm. In order for Christians to attain God's character, we have to be able to first obtain his eyes. What if we loved spiritual reality as much as those Dutch painters loved physical reality? Wouldn't it be interesting if we could see the invisible battle that takes place between the light and dark? Seeing life as it actually is would change our responses…to everything. Our lives would be eternally altered if we saw the people with chains, caused by sin, around their hearts. If we could literally view Satan speaking into someone's ear, maybe we'd be quicker to respond, more passionate to love, and faster to share truth.

Later, in the 1800's, when painting styles merged into impressionism, people believed that realism was lost. It was harder to see reality through the clash of colors. However, when they looked close enough, they could see that the details of reality were still there. Likewise, it's difficult to see what's occurring in the spiritual realm. That's why paying attention is important. Satan tries to tempt us to believe that life would be easier if we'd ignore the truth. When you live blinded to the spiritual realm, it's not just you dying spiritually, but it's the whole world dying spiritually. Hosea 4:6 describes the importance of awareness: "*my people are destroyed from lack of knowledge...*"

So, what is really going on? If we can't *see* spiritual reality, then we can't define it, right? Wrong. God, in his heavenly brilliance, made the characteristics of the natural realm reveal the spiritual realm. You can recognize spiritually poor people by the way they act (haughty, rude, uncontrolled), by their words (bitter, foul, angry), and by their attitudes (prideful, judgmental, negative). Their actions reveal that their hearts are homeless, hungry, and hurting. They are children who are lost and away from their father (in heaven). They operate as orphans—they look for food in dumpsters. The dumpsters of the world are bars, clubs, and parties. These children are cold—their hearts are frozen, and their attitudes are bitterly arctic. They need blankets (God's arms) to keep them warm. They are people with no direction, no Holy Spirit inside them, and no truth.

Unfortunately, the human temptation is to shun them. Displaying compassion isn't easy. However, Jesus never told you to loathe people who deal with sex and drug addictions, people who are unrelenting in their party scene, and those who are steeped in materialism. You might disapprove of their way of life, but their way of life tells you something about their spiritual walk that should provoke you to be concerned for them. You can't win people for God if you have a crinkled nose at their lives. They don't need anyone to belittle them. Satan has given them more despair than they can handle, and that's *why* they are overwhelmed with carnal behaviors. If we hate them, who will reach them? If you flinch at their curse words, spit on their parties, and show disgust for their lives, how can they believe that you are love? And if they don't view you as loving, how can they believe that God loves them? You weren't called to despise the unsaved; you were called to assist in *revitalizing* them. "*...Mercy triumphs over judgment*" (James 2:13). If you're going to share your life with God, you need to share in his desires as well, and his desire is for his people. Before Jesus could come and save us through his death, he had to first have a compassionate heart for us. He knew and was submitted to his mission. "*For the Son of Man came to seek and to save the lost*" (Luke 19:10). Overflowing with compassion will urge you to ambitious *action*. Being concerned for someone's salvation will prompt you to share the gospel with them.

A while ago, a good friend of mine informed me that he would be going to the dance clubs after work. As he began to walk away, I pulled him back to my desk. I squeezed his hand and told him that God loved him. He looked at me for a moment, smiled, and replied, "Okay." I wasn't exactly sure what he'd do that night, but the next day at work he admitted that he didn't go to the bars. He said that he knew he didn't need to go.

My friend's emptiness was replaced with fulfilling truth. God is the *filler*. God was faithful to pull my friend to him by using his loving-kindness. It was the same loving-kindness of God that drew you and, since you are the reflection of God, it will be your loving-kindness that draws others. "*Therefore, as God's chosen people, holy and dearly loved, clothe yourselves with compassion, kindness, humility, gentleness and patience*" (Colossians 3:12).

When reaching those who don't know Christ, remember that God aches as much for the people who are dealing with porn addictions as he does for people in the jungles. If you feel anything else than brokenness for individuals who are pursuing unrighteousness, there may be a problem with your compassion meter. Many are taught from a young age to have compassion on people who are underprivileged. It's looked highly upon when one gives to charities, fundraisers, food drives, and nonprofit organizations. But the world doesn't instruct you to have much empathy for the *spiritual* condition of others.

Ask God to open your spiritual eyes, to break your heart for the spiritual homelessness of others, and to reveal to you the best way you can reach them. Don't be afraid to relate with them. God was continuously drawing you while you were still in darkness. Now it's your turn to be a light to those who are in the dark. Ask God for divine love and brokenness; then ask God to pierce your heart with compassion for the nations. This is the type of brokenness that wins because love wins. If you're going to have a spiritual fashion, let it be compassion!

"So from now on we regard no one from a worldly point of view. Though we once regarded Christ in this way, we do so no longer. Therefore, if anyone is in Christ, he is a new creation; the old has gone, the new has come! All this is from God, who reconciled us to himself through Christ and gave us the ministry of reconciliation: that God was reconciling the world to himself in Christ, not counting men's sins against them. And he has committed to us the message of reconciliation. We are therefore Christ's ambassadors, as though God were making his appeal through us. We implore you on Christ's behalf: Be reconciled to God. God made him who had no sin to be sin for us, so that in him we might become the righteousness of God" (2 Corinthians 5: 16-21).

Application:

Is there someone whose actions you disapprove of? What are things they do that you dislike?

_____

_____

_____

_____

_____

_____

_____

_____

_____

_____

_____

_____

Are there other specific areas of people's lives that provoke you to be uncompassionate? How do you tend to act when you disapprove of someone's lifestyle?

_____

_____

_____

_____

_____

_____

_____

_____

_____

What realization do you need to come to in order to trade your anger at them for compassion?

_____

_____

_____

_____

_____

_____

_____

_____

_____

_____

Start practicing compassion today! Let loving-kindness flow from you so the world will know there is a God who loves them. Remember that compassion is a continuous cultivating of your heart. I encourage you to make the character of compassion an unceasing goal. When you determine your heart to do a sifting, then your eyes do a *shifting*, and you will be able to more clearly see the internal and the eternal.

> # Verse to Remember: *"Carry each other's burdens, and in this way you will fulfill the law of Christ"* (Galatians 6:2).
>
> # Quote to Consider: Remember that even Jesus' most scathing denunciation - a blistering diatribe against the religious leaders of Jerusalem in Matthew 23 - ends with Christ weeping over Jerusalem. Compassion colored everything He did. – John MacArthur[2]

Now, I implore you as a soldier of Jesus Christ, fight *the good fight...finish the race...*keep *the faith* (2 Timothy 4:7).

Day 3

Your Personal Account
Theme: Preparing Your Testimony

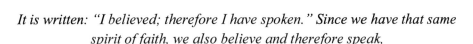

It is written: "I believed; therefore I have spoken." Since we have that same spirit of faith, we also believe and therefore speak,
2 Corinthians 4:13

Four hundred years passed, and God hadn't spoken. This occurred during the time between the Old and New Testament, referred to as the Inter-testamental period. However, God was not idle during those four hundred years; he used that time for preparation of what would come in the future: a massive movement of the gospel throughout the world. God was busy preparing the way for Christ. From 800-500 B.C, Greek colonies were established in several countries and then "extended…over the entire area from the Eastern Mediterranean to the Indus River."[1] The expansion of the Greek culture familiarized all people with the Greek language, which ultimately made it easier to share the gospel. God also prepared Christ's coming through the political advancement of the Romans. The Romans "united the Mediterranean world, permitting an easy flow of people across the entire region…"[2] Therefore, when it came time for Jesus and his disciples to fully expand the gospel, they would have a path to walk on. And God was already moving in the religious scene, making sure that synagogues were being built all throughout the Roman Empire. This gave a jump-start to reaching the gentiles.[3]

Noting that God prepared the timing for Christ is an example of the character he desires for his people: God wants us to be prepared. The concept of preparation is a part of all facets of successful living. If you have a presentation at school or for your career, you will work hard to make sure that it sounds flawless, precise, and eloquent. When you have people over for dinner, you assemble the meal, clean your house, and may set out a game. Being a prepared person should also merge onto the mission field. If you are prepared for physical, temporal activities, then surely you would want to be ready for spiritual, eternal activities. God desires that you be prepared in your spiritual ministry. *"But in your hearts set apart Christ as Lord. Always be prepared to give an answer to everyone who asks you to give the reason for the hope that you have. But do this with gentleness and respect"* (1 Peter 3:15).

The value of having a ready testimony is often overlooked. Your testimony is your account, your experience, and your evidence of the way Christ has moved in your life. When presenting your testimony, you are unveiling a reason for your certainty in Christ; the dying world needs to hear it! Those who are without a relationship with the Father *need* to be able to recognize that you are aware and certain of what God has done in your life.

Think of your testimony as your appeal to the people who don't know Christ. It's your case. Picture a jury intently listening to an attorney plead his case. They cling to every word that he says because they want to see if he has proof to fight for his cause. In the same way, you are the attorney in the spiritual court room, and the people who don't know Christ are the jury. Your experiences are your witnesses; call them to the stand, interrogate them, and pull out of them the *"reason for the hope you have"* (1 Peter 3:15). Other people need to know what God has done in your life. They want to know *why* they should put their faith in God. Don't be afraid to share your story with them; people were created to relate. You can be a part of showing them why you love the Lord. You were meant to be the *"light of the world"* (Matthew 5:14). You were meant to be the unhidden city on the *"hill"* (Matthew 5:14).

In Acts 22, the Apostle Paul stood in front of a large crowd and shared his testimony. He courageously gave an account of where he came from, how he met God, and the things God appointed him to do. Paul gives his account again in Acts 26. It's interesting to note that he uses the same method of explanation as he did the first time. The reason for his repetition is that he was *prepared.* Paul was ready. He knew what he wanted to say, and he said it. He recognized that when he received an opportunity to speak about God his testimony had better be formulated. Paul viewed all Christians as *"ambassadors"* of God: *"We are therefore Christ's ambassadors, as though God were making his appeal through us..."* (2 Corinthians 5:20).

Keep in mind that sharing your testimony is part of what it means to overcome the darkness. Satan has a plan about the things he wants to whisper in people's ears every day. That's why getting ready to have an effective testimony is vital; you want to counteract the words they are hearing from the enemy of their souls. The Bible says in Revelation 12: 10-11 that you can conquer the enemy by knowing your testimony, and it's your testimony that helps you overcome: *"Then I heard a loud voice in heaven say: 'Now have come the salvation and the power and the kingdom of our God, and the authority of his Christ. For the accuser of our brothers, who accuses them before our God day and night, has been hurled down. They overcame him by the blood of the Lamb and by the word of their testimony..."*

Here is some space to journal about your spiritual journey and formulate your testimony.

- First, ask God to bring to your mind the things that he might want to say through you. Are there specific memories that God is bringing to your mind even now?

  _____

  _____

  _____

  _____

  _____

- Then answer the following questions:
  - Where were you emotionally, physically, and spiritually before Christ? What was your life like? What was something specific you struggled with?
  - When did you first realize the love of God? What changed your view of God?
- Next write a list of things you've experienced once you came into Christianity. What are some differences you saw in yourself? Remember that as Paul preached, he used detailed attributes of God.

List bullet points of *specific* instances where God has been faithful… Having several different ways God has moved is useful because they will readily come to mind as opportunities present themselves. Some of you may have entered Christianity at a young age and might not have remembrance of a time without God. So write about how God has proved strong in difficult situations in your life. Make bullet points of the ways God has helped you overcome temptations, mindsets, and sin.

- o

- o

- o

- o

- o

- o

- Finally, if you could end your testimony with one point about who God is to you, what attribute would you use to describe God?

_____

_____

_____

_____

_____

_____

_____

Once you've formulated your points, write the entire outline into complete sentences. Make sure you avoid churchy terms such as *born again*, *sin*, and *lost*; you want an unchurched person to understand what you are talking about. I encourage you to memorize your testimony so that it's at the forefront of your mind. Here is space to rewrite your testimony in full:

Watch and listen to the person you are sharing with. Maybe ask them questions about things they've been through. You may have similar experiences; use those to relate to them. Tell them what God has done on your behalf. This will help you to connect with the unsaved and to form a trust relationship with them. People long to be understood. In closing your testimony, be sensitive to the Spirit of God wanting you to offer them the salvation message.

Final encouragement:

Remember that your account is the greatest story that someone can hear. God knows the exact persons who need to hear from you. The things in your life that you've walked through, lived through, suffered through, the hard times, the good times, the times where you thought you weren't going to make it through the day, the times when you wondered what your purpose was, the times of great faith, and of depression and doubt. These are all part of the ground works of God and you—the love story, the tale of his sovereignty, faithfulness, and unchanging desire for you to be a part of his life.

Verse to Remember: *I will come and proclaim your mighty acts, Sovereign LORD; I will proclaim your righteous deeds, yours alone* (Psalm 71:16).

Quote to Consider: Our lives begin to end the day we become silent about things that matter. –Martin Luther King, Jr.[4]

Now, I implore you as a soldier of Jesus Christ, fight *the good fight...finish the race...*keep *the faith* (2 Timothy 4:7).

Day 4

Going Gallantly

Theme: Authoritative Preaching

...the one who is in you is greater than the one who is in the world.

1 John 4:4

They knew something was different about him. The crowds listened intently as he spoke and read the scriptures. They heard an unusual tone in his voice, a new inflection— *"The people were amazed at his teaching, because he taught them as one who had authority, not as the teachers of the law"* (Mark 1:22). They heard the difference between one who spoke with power and those who did not. In the same way, people we witness to will be able to detect the authority of God in our voices.

Being bold in sharing one's testimony is a common fear. It's hard to tell someone truth when we think they might shun us. It's easy to feel put on the spot or all alone. Unfortunately, we can have our testimonies prepared and never actually utilize them. Normally, the lack of sharing God's work in our lives evolves from fear. We want to be sure that people will believe us or like us. But Jesus wasn't concerned with what people thought. Although masses of people were amazed at Jesus' teaching, many others questioned where he received the power to speak as he did. Jesus was able to respond with surety about his testimony; *"Jesus answered, 'Even if I testify on my own behalf, my testimony is valid, for I know where I came from and where I am going..."* (John 8:14). Jesus knew he was given authority from his all-mighty Father. He even proclaimed, " *'Do you think I cannot call on my Father, and he will at once put at my disposal more than twelve legions of angels?"* (Matthew 26:53). Jesus knew exactly who he was. He knew that he was the life all men needed.

Jesus was able to fulfill his role, his rights, and his call because he knew "*where*" he was "*from and where*" he was "*going*". Keep in mind that evil also knows who you are in Christ (Mark 1:24). If Satan knows it, then how much more should you grasp it?! If you know your role, then you will be able to fill it. You must realize who you are. You, dear fanatic, have been called an heir, the light, and a victor.

- You are an heir:

  An heir to a throne is marked with privileges: privileges of power and authority. Galatians 3:29 says, "*If you belong to Christ, then you are Abraham's seed, and heirs according to the promise.*" You get to have the say- so in the lives of others that will launch a cause and effect movement—where the cause is the love of God and the effect is changed, renewed lives. An heir also tends to the work of the King. When Jesus was only twelve years old, he stayed in the temple area. When his parents found him, Jesus said that he was doing his "*Father's business*" (Luke 2:49 KJV). Jesus was talking about doing the work of his heavenly Father. He knew that he was God's son. You also are God's child, and therefore you are equipped with the same Spirit as Jesus Christ! Romans 8:16-17 reveals that, "*The Spirit himself testifies with our spirit that we are God's children. Now if we are children, then we are heirs—heirs of God and co-heirs with Christ, if indeed we share in his sufferings in order that we may also share in his glory.*"

- You are the light:

  1 Thessalonians 5:5 says, "*You are all children of the light and children of the day. We do not belong to the night or to the darkness.*"

  On November 5, 1815, a young lady was born who would shake history in Britain. Her name was Grace Darling. She grew up in a lighthouse in Northumberland, where her father was the keeper. It was early in the morning on September 7, 1838, when Grace gazed out an upstairs window upon a raging storm. There she witnessed a shipwreck and countless people drowning. She determinedly prepared to rescue those who were fighting for their lives. She and her father, William, rushed to their aid. With only a rowboat out upon hazardous waters, they paddled nearly one mile, fighting the waves in order to reach the people. Grace saved five townspeople and four sailors. She even rescued a woman who was holding two of her dead children.[1]

Grace knew that she had a father who was the lighthouse keeper. In the same way, God is the light and you are of him. Just as Grace boldly went out on the sea, God has called you to be bold in your declaration of his love. Grace Darling came from the lighthouse and in the same way, you come from the light (Psalm 18:28).

- You are a victor:

As you battle for people's souls, keep in mind the promise that God made to his people when they went to battle: *"Be strong and courageous. Do not be afraid or terrified because of them, for the LORD your God goes with you; he will never leave you nor forsake you"* (Deuteronomy 31: 6). You were molded to exude courage. 1 Corinthians 6:17 says, *"But he who unites himself with the Lord is one with him in spirit,"* and 2 Timothy 1:7 reveals that *"…the Spirit God gave us does not make us timid, but gives us power, love and self-discipline."*

Toleration for trepidation is a tragic postponement of your faith and of your effectiveness. Remember that exuding boldness is an influential mechanism for your victory over Satan. It tells the story of who you are just as it did for Peter and John in Acts 4:13: *"When they saw the courage of Peter and John and realized that they were unschooled, ordinary men, they were astonished and they took note that these men had been with Jesus."* It was Peter's and John's passion for God that drove them to boldness and action for the cause of Christ: *"For we cannot help speaking about what we have seen and heard'"* (Acts 4:20).

Understanding that fear comes from lies and not from love has assisted me in my call to witness. Truth is hard to say sometimes. It isn't easy to communicate because it doesn't always sound *appealing*. But God's truth usually isn't politically correct. Absolute truth was never promised to echo with charm. However, you can still preach with love and authority because you know that you are an heir, the light, and a victor through the one who loves you! Dread defiles and distracts one's devotion to the truth. The enemy's lies about what will happen if you choose to share the gospel operate as a roadblock to boldness.

Think of Satan like a scarecrow sitting in the fields of harvest. He wants to frighten you, in hopes that you will run away from reaping the harvest (Kingdom of God). However, remember that Satan only holds power through your agreeable acknowledgment of his lies. Real power was stripped away from Satan when Jesus gave his life. Yet Satan is determined to hassle you, hoping that he'll watch you break. But he is a deceiver who likes to flash his unflattering face. The only authority he can even hope to clutch is the ability to cause you to fear. But you choose fear. Satan can't *make* you be afraid; he can only *tempt* you to be troubled.

You were molded to be a fearless fanatic for the cause of Christ. Take all your hesitations to Jesus. Share your account! Be confident about it! Even if you have people mock, laugh at, or speak against your testimony, you can be bold because *you know* who you are. Rise up in Christ's confidence and go gallantly, heir of God, warrior of light, unbreakable victor.

Application:

Take some time to look at how you've dealt with being outspoken about God in the past. Pray that God will reveal to you issues you may have with being active in sharing your faith.

Take a moment to hone in on the times when you have shied away from sharing the gospel; what thoughts were swirling in your head? What fears were you struggling with? What lies do you think Satan told you in order to keep you from sharing the truth?

_____

_____

_____

_____

_____

_____

_____

_____

How does understanding who you are in Christ derail Satan's endeavors to bring you fear?

_____

_____

_____

_____

_____

_____

_____

_____

God calls you an heir, the light, and a victor; which one speaks to you the most, and why?

_____

_____

_____

_____

_____

_____

Keep in mind who you are in Christ, and go gallantly.

Verse to **R**emember: *If the ministry that condemns men is glorious, how much more glorious is the ministry that brings righteousness! For what was glorious has no glory now in comparison with the surpassing glory. And if what was fading away came with glory, how much greater is the glory of that which lasts! Therefore, since we have such a hope, we are very bold* (2 Corinthians 3: 9-12).

Quote to **C**onsider: Activate yourself to duty by remembering your position, who you are, and what you have obliged yourself to be. –Thomas Kempis[2]

Now, I implore you as a soldier of Jesus Christ, fight *the good fight...finish the race...*keep *the faith* (2 Timothy 4:7).

Day 5

Ditching Death

Theme: Leaving Bitterness Behind

... "If your enemy is hungry, feed him; if he is thirsty, give him something to drink. In doing this, you will heap burning coals on his head." Do not be overcome by evil, but overcome evil with good.

Romans 12:20-21

Part of maintaining successful warrior living is looking at your heart and making sure that you hold no grievances against anyone. As you continue to think about being active in sharing your testimony, keep in mind that it's easier to be effective when your heart is free from contempt or bitterness. It's pretty difficult to help set captives free if you're the one who is captive. Before you step your feet onto someone's territory to reveal Christ to them, make sure your heart is totally right toward the people in your life. Although it may be hard to mend the relationship before you go out on missions, it is necessary that you deal with any unforgiveness in yourself.

When God called you out of the darkness and into the light, he never expected that you would take the darkness with you. Ephesians 5:8 says, *"For you were once darkness, but now you are light in the Lord. Live as children of light."* It's important to know what to leave behind in a spiritual sense. It's vital to know that your internal feelings and struggles will influence your effectiveness on the mission field, and it can also affect the amount of revival you experience for yourself. You want to be free from burdensome situations so you can fully focus on the task at hand—sharing

God's love with the world. Forgiveness is about being pure of heart. Matthew 5:8 says that those who are *"pure of heart"* will *"see God"*. If you are unable to see the Lord, you cannot fully know the Lord; if you don't fully know him, it will be much more difficult to be a witness of him.

God calls you to love others more than they are able to love you. Essentially, he is asking you to be just as he is—he is asking you to be *"holy"* (1 Peter 1:16). God loves you more than you could ever love him, and he does not hold grudges against humanity, even though he has been wronged. We've all been forgiven for something, haven't we? It's an amazing feeling to receive undeserved forgiveness *because* forgiveness is so hard to bestow. It's especially hard to forgive people when they purposefully aim darts of hatred your way. When someone has taken you for granted, cursed you, gossiped, lied about you, turned on you, and done everything in their power to hurt you, love gets rough. If the pain wasn't so bad, if the words didn't sting so much, if the knife which stabbed through your emotions didn't pierce so deeply, then maybe you'd be able to forgive them, right? Wrong. The intensity of their hatred doesn't give exemptions for you to have personal vendettas. Your love *has* to outdo their actions, or else you aren't really conquering the battle of love.

You're called to be fanatically forgiving! You were appointed to dispense a pure pardoning of being wronged. Love holds no wrongs (1 Corinthians 13). Leviticus 19:18 says *""Do not seek revenge or bear a grudge against one of your people, but love your neighbor as yourself. I am the LORD."* What does vengeance look like played out in real life? It looks like purposeful plots, sour sarcasm, and callous glances. Essentially, vengeance looks like hate. If you choose revenge, it means that you've forgotten something about God which he promised he would be: your *avenger*. Romans12:19 says, *"Do not take revenge, my friends, but leave room for God's wrath, for it is written: 'It is mine to avenge; I will repay,' says the Lord."*

Although God is your defender, he does have an opinion about those who treat you poorly—he hates that you would suffer by human hands. Understanding God means understanding that he delights in defending you. He delights in seeing you succeed, and he can save you from harm. *"Commit your way to the LORD; trust in him and he will do this: He will make your righteousness shine like the dawn, the justice of your cause like the noonday sun. Be still before the LORD and wait patiently for him; do not fret when men succeed in their ways, when they carry out their wicked schemes"*

(Psalm 37:5-7).

Waiting on God to defend you does not permit you to bear grudges in the meantime. Grudges aren't optional for warrior living. It's tempting to forgive based on satisfaction that God may be vindictive in dealing with them. It may be true that God will confront them for what they did to you, but your attitude toward the situation needs to demonstrate the characteristics of God. Gloating that others might have to go through misery on account of their wrongdoing is not forgiveness; that's *vengeance*. That's the kind of attitude God rebuked Jonah for possessing.

Jonah, an Old Testament prophet, didn't want to go to the city of Nineveh to deliver the message of repentance. He knew that if the people chose to repent, God would forgive them. We don't know for sure why Jonah was so apprehensive about God's forgiveness; maybe Jonah had lost family or friends in the Ninevite attacks. Whatever it was, it's obvious that he gloried in the idea of God destroying them.

"He prayed to the Lord, 'O LORD, is this not what I said when I was still at home? That is why I was so quick to flee to Tarshish. I knew that you are a gracious and compassionate God, slow to anger and abounding in love, a God who relents from sending calamity" (Jonah 4:2). Jonah ignored God's unchanging idea about who the battle is really against: *"For our struggle is not against flesh and blood, but against the rulers, against the authorities, against the powers of this dark world and against the spiritual forces of evil in the heavenly realms"* (Ephesians 6:12).

Abraham Lincoln is famous for saying, "Am I not destroying my enemies when I make friends of them?"[1] He was right! The goal is not to destroy people. The idea is to destroy the authorities of the evil realm. Satan longs for broken relationships. How can your heart be right before God if you are wishing disaster upon someone who hurt you? The entire point of forgiveness is so that you can better reflect God.

What does Micah 7:18 say about what God delights to do?

_____

_____

How has this affected you in your own life? Can you think of a time when God has used this attribute with you?

_____

_____

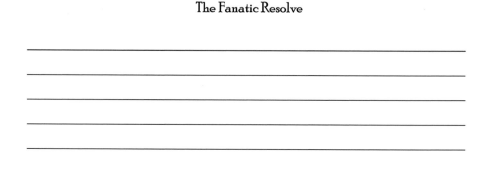

It's tempting to feel alone in the battle to forgive, but forgiveness is historical. It's not an attribute only our generation has had to deal with. Since the beginning of time, people have faced the battle to forgive. One of them was a young man named Joseph, who was undeservedly mistreated by his brothers. They mocked his dreams, laughed at his visions, threw him in a pit, sold him into slavery, and even told their father, Jacob, that Joseph was dead (Genesis 37). But when an opportune time came for Joseph to take revenge, this is how he responded: " *His brothers then came and threw themselves down before him. 'We are your slaves,' they said. But Joseph said to them, 'Don't be afraid. Am I in the place of God? You intended to harm me, but God intended it for good to accomplish what is now being done, the saving of many lives. So then, don't be afraid. I will provide for you and your children.' And he reassured them and spoke kindly to them*" (Genesis 50:18-21).

Joseph fulfilled his duty to be fanatically forgiving. Joseph was able to forgive because he saw that when the battle to love those who mistreat you is achieved God gets the glory. Not only did Joseph choose to forgive his brothers, but he actually ended up taking care of them and their children! That just adds a whole other element to the idea of forgiveness. Jesus talked about this component as well; it's defined as blessing those who harm you (Luke 6:28).

I had a friend steal from me once, and when I asked God what to do, he brought this verse to mind: "*And if anyone wants to sue you and take your shirt, hand over your coat as well*" (Matthew 5:40). My immediate response was, "No way!" God was asking me to not only let them have what they took, but if they wanted something else to freely give it to them. God awakened my heart to the powerful truth that humanity stole from God the pure relationship he wanted with us. Then not only did he give his Son on our cross, but he offers us salvation… for "*free*" (Revelations 22:17).

In the end, people who harm you will see the way you respond to them, and that will be a witness to them. After David forgave Saul for trying to kill him, Saul's response to David was: "*'You are more righteous than I,' he said. 'You have treated me well, but I have treated you badly. You have just now told me of the good you did to me; the LORD delivered me into your hands, but you did not kill me. When a man finds his enemy, does he let him get away unharmed? May the LORD reward you well for the way you treated me today*" (1 Samuel 24:17-19).

Keep in mind that, as you forgive others, you will in turn be blessed. "*Do not repay evil with evil or insult with insult, but with blessing, because to this you were called so that you may inherit a blessing*" (1 Peter 3:9). Remember to leave behind bitterness and take up the cross of forgiveness. You must ditch death (unforgiveness) in order to be fully entwined with a pure and holy life.

Application:

As you answer each question, ask God to reveal your heart to you and to search the places in your mind that you keep hidden.

Is there a hurtful situation that has clung to the walls of your mind for a long time? What are your feelings toward the person(s) who hurt you?

_____

_____

_____

_____

_____

_____

_____

_____

_____

_____

_____

_____

_____

_____

_____

How do you foresee that situation keeping you from effective ministry? Have you noticed it already damaging ministry for you in the past? How?

_____

_____

_____

_____

_____

_____

_____

How does it make you feel to know that God desires you to forgive the one(s) who hurt you?

_____

_____

_____

_____

_____

_____

_____

_____

_____

_____

_____

_____

Pray that God helps you to forgive them. Then ask God to fill you with the prayers they need prayed over them. What are those prayers he's asking you to pray?

_____

_____

_____

_____

_____

_____

_____

_____

_____

_____

Do you think it will take more than prayer in order to provoke forgiveness for them in your heart? If so, what is something you can commit yourself to doing for them?

_____

_____

_____

_____

_____

If you don't know what to do, maybe buy them a little gift or send them a card. Do something that will defeat the enemy's desire for conflict. Love softens hearts (Proverbs 18:16). Remember to get your heart right before you go out to witness. Make sure that God's love is fully ruling in your life, so you and your ministry can be totally uninhibited, totally free.

Verse to Remember: *Bear with each other and forgive whatever grievances you may have against one another. Forgive as the Lord forgave you* (Colossians 3:13).

Quote to Consider: Forgiveness does not change the past, but it does enlarge the future. –Paul Boese[2]

Now, I implore you as a soldier of Jesus Christ, fight *the good fight...finish the race...*keep *the faith* (2 Timothy 4:7).

Day 6

The Way We Tread

Theme: Being Sensitive to Diverse Cultures

How beautiful on the mountains are the feet of those who bring good news, who proclaim peace, who bring good tidings, who proclaim salvation, who say to Zion, "Your God reigns!"

Isaiah 52:7

It was midafternoon. The sun had started to go down in the city of Brasov, Romania. A travel buddy and I just wanted a warm coffee before we would head up onto the highest point of the city. We ventured into a small coffee shop and as we walked in the oddest sight struck us—there were kilts hanging all over the walls. I figured that the Romanian who ran the coffee shop just liked kilts. So I, being somewhat of a jokester, referred to the kilts as "mini dresses," and I'm pretty sure I continued to go on about men who wear skirts. Clearly, I thought it was funny. However, the *English-speaking* Scottish gentleman behind the counter did not. I had no idea he spoke English, no idea that he was Scottish. I was the opposite side of Europe! I then became the object of his fury, and he would not let the subject go about the fact that I had made fun of his culture. He even raised the price of my coffee. Yes, it is true. I had to pay more for the coffee because he was incredibly upset with me. He said, "Seven Leu, a special price for you…"

I probably deserved his harsh scolding. His first comment to me was, "If a Scot heard you say that he would put up a fight." It's easy to forget that we don't know everything that is going on around us. It never occurred to me that a Scottish man would pick up his whole life and move to Romania to sell coffee. But, it didn't matter. I should not have made jokes that could offend other people. It's true that people tend to be insensitive if they aren't aware of other cultures. When entering into other people's lives, you never know what they have been through emotionally or spiritually, and you also don't know what their humor is like.

The beginning verse for today's devotional was Isaiah 52:7 which stated, *"How beautiful on the mountains are the feet of those who bring good news, who proclaim peace, who bring good tidings, who proclaim salvation, who say to Zion, "Your God reigns!"* It wouldn't be very beautiful if one were to enter into another person's territory, tell them about Jesus, and then insult every detail of their life. I will be the first to tell you that I've failed miserably several times with being sensitive to other people. I disregarded the truth that when Christ came to earth, he didn't focus on the physical nature of mankind; he came to find and revive what was *spiritually* lost (Luke 19:10). In the same way, you have been called to extend the news of Christ to shine into the darkness. However, while proclaiming God's truth, remember that all things outside of scripture, such as personal opinions, were never meant to be the main focus of God's message. When you engage in conversation with someone, you will encounter their world view. Part of reaching those who don't know Christ is doing all things in love. You can talk about Christ without insulting their beliefs, their ideas, and their culture. Having beautiful feet is ultimately treading with humility, understanding, and kindness. *"...slander no one, to be peaceable and considerate, and always to be gentle toward everyone"* (Titus 3:2).

"...slander no one..." and tread with humility. 1 Corinthians 10:12 says, *"So, if you think you are standing firm, be careful that you don't fall!"* Sometimes pride comes in like a thief and steals the purity of humility. It's easy to be critical of other cultures and people when you didn't grow up the same way they did. But don't drink the jaded juice of judgment; pride has no place in the story of redemption. There is no room for spiritual or cultural pride. I have found myself falling into a cycle of pride that somehow my culture was much more advanced. I needed a hearty wake-up call: nobody is better than anybody else. Personal preferences are *different*, not *better*. Every culture is unique.

"...*be peaceable and considerate*..." and tread with understanding. New places can be refreshing, relaxing, and restoring. Getting away from daily routine can be adventuresome and life changing. But unfamiliar settings can also be a rude awakening. God didn't call you to change other people's amoral habits. He called you to make an impact on their *hearts*. He didn't call you to tell them what you really think about the taste of their food. He called you to tell them how much God loves them. When reaching out, anticipate the art of adjustment. If you are going on international missions, expect shocking sights, diverse smells, unusual tastes, unique clothes, and bizarre bugs. You might be extremely uncomfortable. But, maintain consideration. God knew before you were born that he would call you to locations and situations that weren't the most comfortable, and yet he still called you to be "*peaceable and considerate.*"

"...*always be gentle toward everyone*..." and tread with kindness. While misunderstandings can be humorous, a lot of times they can be hurtful. Watch words, clothes, and body language. Other people's ideas about what is lovely may seem strange to you. But, I assure you, you seem abnormal to them as well. You're walking into their lives. As long as the things they are doing aren't unbiblical, then their different tastes shouldn't be something that you are concerned about. Maybe you can even learn from them. Learn to value what they value. Let them show you what their lives are like. You just show them Christ.

If you're focusing on the spiritual, then the physical won't be an immense ordeal. It would be wise for you to major on the majors, and the only true major is showing them the love of Christ. "*For the kingdom of God is not a matter of eating and drinking, but of righteousness, peace and joy in the Holy Spirit ,Let us therefore make every effort to do what leads to peace and to mutual edification. Do not destroy the work of God for the sake of food*..." (Romans 14: 17, 19-20). Does that mean that you can't observe and celebrate the many traditions of another society? Of course not! That's one of the beauties of travel. Just don't allow the temporary, tangible, outward things to divert you from your mission.

I encourage you to steady your mind. Be a fanatic for the souls you encounter, when you meet new people with different world views. If you want to follow Christ's footsteps, then it is essential that you learn to love others straight through their exterior. Having an *eternal* perspective versus the *external* perspective is vital when it comes to the cause of Christ. The type of love that God has taught you in his Word is not fleeting. God's love is purposed to be eternally and fundamentally fulfilling.

The most important key to entering another culture is learning to feel the way that Jesus feels for them—being able to look past cultural differences and look directly at their hearts. *"So we fix our eyes not on what is seen, but on what is unseen. For what is seen is temporary, but what is unseen is eternal"* (2 Corinthians 4:18).

Application:

What you experience physically can cause you to react insensitively. The way you tread through their lives can be insulting if you aren't aware of your comfort zones.

Recognize your preferences. It is vital that you distinguish these, so you won't be surprised by the possible overwhelming feeling of discomfort. Identify what personal preferences you have that might get in the way of ministry. What are the things you enjoy most about home?

_____

_____

_____

_____

_____

_____

When do you experience the most physical discomfort?

_____

_____

_____

_____

_____

_____

_____

_____

What is one thing you think you could not survive without daily?

_____

_____

_____

_____

_____

_____

What are your food preferences, cleanliness preferences, and sleep preferences?

_____

_____

_____

_____

_____

_____

Think about and write down your inclinations. The next step is to smash them! Demolishing your preferential zones is committing yourself to be above reproach in uncomfortable situations. It's when you resolve to remain active in being content, thankful, and humble.

Identify tempting topics: What topics do you think you should avoid while you're on a trip in order to not offend?

_____

_____

_____

_____

_____

_____

_____

_____

_____

_____

_____

Identify motives for what you take with you on your journey. Pray about your clothes, your hobbies, and your intentions. Is there anything in your suitcase that you may need to leave at home or get rid of before you enter the field?

You are clay, going to a people who are clay, to reach into their hearts - which are created to be eternal.

Verse to Remember: _Do nothing out of selfish ambition or vain conceit. Rather, in humility value others above yourselves,_ (Philippians 2:3).

Quote to Consider: Both gentleness and meekness are born of power, not weakness. There is a pseudo-gentleness that is effeminate, and there is a pseudo-meekness that is cowardly. But a Christian is to be gentle and meek because those are Godlike virtues... Jerry Bridges[1]

Now, I implore you as a soldier of Jesus Christ, fight _the good fight...finish the race...keep the faith_ (2 Timothy 4:7).

Day 7

Commissioned to Cry

Theme: Intercession

I call on you, my God, for you will answer me; turn your ear to me and hear my prayer. Show me the wonders of your great love, you who save by your right hand those who take refuge in you from their foes.

Psalm 17:6-7

The foundation of the city was shaking. The people were shouting. Triumph was coming. The walls of the city of Jericho were falling. It was early that morning that the Israelites tramped their feet straight ahead, with no reserve, around the walls of Jericho for the last time. They knew that they would see victory if they would obey the Lord. He had commanded them to walk around Jericho's walls for six days and on the seventh day to walk around the walls seven times while giving a great shout. God had promised that the walls would come falling down for their triumph. And his promise came true (Joshua 5-6).

It's important to note that God called the Israelites to action *several times* before they saw the *result* of their obedience. Likewise, God has called us to be obedient to intercession. God calls us to begin our march of prayer for others far before we will actually see the walls of depression, darkness, and despair come tumbling down. The enemy wants to cage people into cities of hopelessness, shame, and confusion. However those city walls of the enemy are not sturdy when God's people pray against them. Now is the time to begin to conquer those walls. We can begin to conquer those city walls through the power of prayer. Just as the Lord longed to deliver the city of Jericho into the hands of the Israelites for his glory, God also longs to entrust us with people to pray for.

Jesus understood that praying in advance for people was powerful (John 17). Oh, I wish I could have heard it—I wonder what it sounded like when he prayed. I wonder if his words were rattled with solemnity. Maybe unstoppable tears flowed down his somber cheeks. Maybe he gazed ahead with deep concern creviced between his brows. Could you image wiping the tears of Christ? Having his emotion on your fingers, and maybe even catching his tears on your shirt? It would be an incomparable honor to hold Jesus while he cried and to let your clothing be the napkin that dried his eyes.

Hearing God's heart coming through Christ's prayers would have been transforming. Even though we cannot physically hear Jesus speak the words he said in the gospels, we know he said them—they aren't any less true, alive, or important. He might not have wept on our shoulders, but he has cried out for our souls.

When Jesus left the earth, he left you equipped with his Spirit. The Spirit's role isn't only to speak to you; he's also there to *pray* for you. Romans 8:27 says, "*And he who searches our hearts knows the mind of the Spirit, because the Spirit intercedes for the saints in accordance with God's will.*" His Spirit is always interceding for us. Therefore, if we belong to him and his Spirit is in us, we will share his passion to pray for others. God is always people minded. God is zealously in love with humanity. It seems odd that such a pure person could be passionately enamored with saving a corrupt people. In a spiritual and literal sense, Jesus came into our dirty world to save us. He came in order to bridge the gap between us and God that we couldn't fill for ourselves. And he wants us to do the same for others.

Praying for other people isn't an *optional* part of Christianity. Intercession isn't a *suggestion*; it's a *command*. God expects his people to pray. Look up Matthew 6:5, 6, and 7. What is the repeated phrase that is used at the beginning of each verse?

Why do you think that Jesus repeated those words? What do you think he meant?

_____

_____

_____

_____

Intercession is lifting someone before the judgment seat of God and asking God to be merciful to them. Judges seem to have a reputation for being feared. But God's ruling is intermingled with his love. The judgment seat of God was not meant to be a scare tactic. Psalm 9:8 reveals attributes God uses when he judges; what are they?

_____

_____

_____

What type of throne does Hebrews 4:16 say God has?

_____

_____

1 John 5:14-15 says, *"This is the confidence we have in approaching God: that if we ask anything according to his will, he hears us. And if we know that he hears us—whatever we ask—we know that we have what we asked of him."* When your prayers align with the word of God, you can be positive that what you are asking God for is perfectly in his will. His word is his agreement; it's his covenant between you and him. God is *subject* to his word, and he desires that all mankind come to know him. Therefore, you can pray for others with full confidence. Remember, God is *always* faithful to do his part.

Application:

As you meet people you want to pray for, you can use these intercessory prayer points as a checklist. Begin right now praying these things over the people you will meet. You can knock down the walls of darkness today!

- Eyes to see: Ask God to open the eyes of those who are spiritually blind. 2 Corinthians 4:3-4 says, *"And even if our gospel is veiled, it is veiled to those who are perishing. The god of this age has blinded the minds of unbelievers, so that they cannot see the light of the gospel of the glory of Christ, who is the image of God."* Ask God to give them 20/20 *spiritual* vision. Ask the Lord to remove spiritual blinders.

- Ears to hear: Ask the Lord to open their spiritual and physical ears. A friend of mine said that when her child was only two he was throwing a horrible tantrum, and she felt like it was evil. So she rebuked Satan's spirit out of her son, and at the age of only *two* he put his little hands over his ears as she prayed. Satan blocking the spiritual and physical hearing of heavenly words is not a joke. Satan will try to block them from noticing your words of life. Pray that God will remove Satan's hands which are over their ears.

- Wisdom and understanding: Pray that they obtain a clear revelation. It is ineffective for them to see and hear if they cannot understand. The Bible says in John 1:5, *"The light shines in the darkness, but the darkness has not understood it."* We know that the darkness is not able to understand the light.

- Recognition of the times: (Luke 19:44, Matthew 16:3). Having a clear vision of the catastrophe of Satan's movements will spur their spirits to chase God. It's vital that they realize the evil days in which we live.

- Soil of their hearts: Luke 8 says that good soil produces the Godly seeds. Ask God to guard the seeds you plant in their lives, that they may be watered and grow. Ask God to ready their hearts for the seeds before you even meet them.

- A divine drawing: Ask God for a radical drawing of their spirits towards you. You already know that you are Jesus to those who are perishing, and look how people responded to him—*"So the Pharisees said to one another, 'See, this is getting us nowhere. Look how the whole world has gone after him!'"* (John 12:19). The entire world was drawn to Jesus because they saw that he was doing miracles. You are the temple of God, and his essence can pour out through you. Pray that people sense that pouring of the Spirit and are drawn to it.

- Harvesters: *"He told them, 'The harvest is plentiful, but the workers are few. Ask the Lord of the harvest, therefore, to send out workers into his harvest field"* (Luke 10:2). Ask God to awaken more Christians to the need of sharing the gospel.

If you don't feel you have the words to pray, then pray scripture. Praying scripture doesn't mean that you have to read each word over them; simply pick out the qualities that you want God to plant in their lives. For example, Ezekiel 36:25-27 says, *"Then I will sprinkle clean water on you, and you will be clean; I will cleanse you from all your impurities and from all your idols. I will give you a new heart and put a new spirit in you; I will remove from you your heart of stone and give you a heart of flesh. And I will put my Spirit in you and move you to follow my decrees and be careful to keep my laws."* Using this verse as a prayer, you can ask God to *"sprinkle clean water"* on them, to *"cleanse from impurities,"* and to give them *"a new heart and put a new spirit."* Pray that God will *"remove"* their *"heart of stone."*

Ask God to burden your intercessor heart for specific people. Remembering people in prayer is the greatest gift you can give to them. You will have the chance to meet many people as you spread the news of the Kingdom of God. Who have you already met that you want to pray for? If you can't remember their names, write down where you met them, and put specifics so you can easily recall your situation. Then add the things you spoke with them about. If you didn't speak with them at all, then write down the things you felt impressed on your spirit to pray for them.

Date :   Person Met:

Story about meeting:

_____

_____

_____

_____

_____

What to pray for them:

-

-

-

-

Date :   Person Met:

Story about meeting:

_____

_____

_____

_____

_____

What to pray for them:

-

-

-

-

(There is an additional prayer log on page 225).

As God works on their hearts and in their lives, ask him to make you aware of it. If he chooses to do so, then journal about it at a later date. It's amazing to watch God answer prayer. This log will help you to remember their names and their situations. Maybe bend down the page, so you have quick access to writing someone's name down or finding someone to pray for. I believe someday you'll be able to write next to their names praises of what God has done.

Remember intercession is effective, even if you can't see it. God is faithful. He will answer as you pray. It is your commission to cry out for them.

> **Verse to Remember:** *The LORD has heard my cry for mercy; the LORD accepts my prayer* (Psalm 6:9).
>
> **Quote to Consider:** If sinners be damned, at least let them leap to Hell over our bodies. If they will perish, let them perish with our arms about their knees. Let no one go there unwarned and unprayed for. – Charles Spurgeon[1]

Now, I implore you as a soldier of Jesus Christ, fight *the good fight…finish the race…*keep *the faith* (2 Timothy 4:7).

Day 8

Growing Gold

Theme: Faith Filled Fanatic

In addition to all this, take up the shield of faith, with which you can extinguish all the flaming arrows of the evil one.

Ephesians 6:16

Around 700 B.C, the Assyrian army had a massive weapon that went ahead of each man in battle—it was a shield. Although the Assyrian nation was not befriended by God's people, we can still admire their weaponry and their preparation for battle. While there are many different shield forms throughout history, the Assyrians army had a unique form— their shields were bigger than the warriors! It extended all the way from their feet and went past their heads. The top of the shield curved inward in order to disperse any arrows of the enemy.[1]

There is another type of shield. It's a spiritual shield with which God has armed you. It's the shield of faith. The first problem with humanity was that we didn't believe God was truthful. It was the beginning of time. The first humans in existence, Adam and Eve, dropped their shield of faith in believing that the Faithful One loved them enough to do what was right on their behalf. Because they dropped their shields, they were unable to withstand the darts of the enemy. The Assyrians understood the tragedy that would occur without their shields, hence their massive structure. In the same way, it is essential for you to contain faith that will outdo you—a shield of faith that is superior to daily, problematic occurrences which come to silence your active, worshipful belief.

Unappealing and unexpected circumstances are Satan's endeavor to squash Godly faith. But God uses those conditions to refine your faith. In the Bible, faith is compared to gold; the Scriptures say that faith, like gold, must be refined (1 Peter 1:7). The process of gold refinement is exhausting. It first has to go through a mini-refinement referred to as "assaying." Holes are drilled into the gold and delivered to the lab. The value of the gold must be agreed upon by the customer and the refiner. If they disagree, the gold has to be returned to the refiner again! Finally, once all contracts are established, the entire gold piece is placed into a furnace where chlorine gas is added. Although the gas has the ability to break the gold, the refiner is careful enough that the gold will not be destroyed. As the gold boils, metals such as silver, nickel, and copper float to the top and are scraped off. Finally, the gold is dunked into a gold-base solution, and then the gold is complete! [2]

Whew! No wonder the longer the process of gold refinement the more valuable the gold! There are several steps to seeing gold become pure. Likewise, God wants to purify your faith, he wants to build it and make it bigger than your circumstance. You may have to go through refinement several times so that your faith can be firmly established. What would be the point of having a shield of faith if your shield was flimsy? God desires that your faith be of value in your life, so that you will know how to approach and battle each situation.

It's not fun to be placed in a situation that can burn. Maybe you feel like you are being prepped for refinement, or right in the middle of watching all your other "metals" come out, or possibly you feel like you're in the chlorine gas. Keep in mind that the refiner is careful with his precious metals, and God is the ultimate refiner (Malachi 3:2-4). He handles you with care. God won't let you be destroyed. He is vigilant with your faith. He wants to turn you into a faith machine, so you can block those darts of the enemy!

There is a beautifully ironic twist to the idea that your shield of faith is like gold. Ephesians 6:16 informs us that the "*shield of faith*" snuffs out "*all the flaming arrows of the evil one.*" How symbolic that Satan is throwing "*flaming arrows*" your way, and your golden shield is refined through fire! Do you see the miracle?! God takes those fiery darts of Satan and uses them to refine you. Just when Satan thinks he is harming you, God takes his weapons and uses them to burn into you a faith that is lasting. "*In all this you greatly rejoice, though now for a little while you may have had to suffer grief in all kinds of trials. These have come so that the proven genuineness of your faith—of greater worth than gold, which perishes even though refined by fire—may result in praise, glory and honor when Jesus Christ is revealed. Though you have not seen him, you love him; and even though you do not see him now, you believe in him and are filled with an inexpressible and glorious joy,"* (1 Peter 1:6-8).

In closing, remember that faith is evident through your response to a circumstance. Flourishing, fanatic faith looks like godly responses to severely tough situations. *"Many will be purified, made spotless and refined, but the wicked will continue to be wicked. None of the wicked will understand, but those who are wise will understand"* (Daniel 12:10).

Application:

What painful, burning circumstance are you currently enduring?

_____

_____

_____

_____

_____

_____

_____

_____

Just like other types of elements came out of the gold, what type of character flaws do you see coming out of you which God is already beginning to scrape away?

_____

_____

_____

_____

_____

_____

_____

_____

Can you think of a time where you went through a tough season and came out with stronger faith? What happened? How did God prove himself?

_____

_____

_____

_____

_____

_____

_____

How does remembering the outcome of past struggles help you in your response to the fire you are currently in?

_____

_____

_____

_____

_____

_____

_____

_____

_____

_____

_____

_____

_____

_____

_____

_____

How are your actions in the situation revealing your trust in God's refinement? Are you letting God refine you during the fire, or are you allowing your faith to be plowed over by the enemy? What is your normal response to dealing with hardship?

_____

_____

_____

_____

_____

_____

_____

How is it symbolic that the Assyrian army created shields of faith bigger than their bodies? How does that fact speak to you about the size of your faith? What would having faith bigger than your circumstance look like for you?

_____

_____

_____

_____

_____

_____

_____

_____

_____

_____

_____

_____

_____

_____

Ask God to help you see how he is working to build your faith. Remember that those darts of the enemy are used to only grow and strengthen you. While in the throes of battle, stand firm, and hold your shield strong until you become a faith filled fanatic!

Verse to Remember: *Dear friends, do not be surprised at the fiery ordeal that has come on you to test you, as though something strange were happening to you. But rejoice inasmuch as you participate in the sufferings of Christ, so that you may be overjoyed when his glory is revealed* (1 Peter 4:12-13).

Quote to Consider: We are always on the anvil; by trials God is shaping us for higher things—Henry Ward Beecher[3]

Now, I implore you as a soldier of Jesus Christ, fight *the good fight...finish the race...*keep *the faith* (2 Timothy 4:7).

Day 9

Just like Bullets

Theme: Those Blasted Thoughts

The weapons we fight with are not the weapons of the world. On the contrary, they have divine power to demolish strongholds. We demolish arguments and every pretension that sets itself up against the knowledge of God, and we take captive every thought to make it obedient to Christ.

2 Corinthians 10:4-5

We prepare our breakfast. We fix our hair. We assemble our outfits. We normally spend more than enough time getting ready for the day, but it's easy to displace the importance of being alert and prepared in our minds. It's tempting to disregard the fact that one's thought life ends up forming one's deeds. But if we want to maintain fanatical living for Christ, we must remember that the actions that accompany one's life are usually a direct result of one's mind. It's inevitable that one will live out what they think about. In order to uphold a godly life, we must maintain godly thoughts. Studies reveal that the number of thoughts a human has in a day is around 70,000.[1] That is a lot of thoughts to try to control! That means that 70,000 times a day you have a choice to let your mind be focused on God. While you are stretching yourself to be more evangelistic with your lifestyle, remember that your thought life will affect the way you minister. Paying attention to your thought life is one aspect of the call to being an alert warrior.

In Judges 7, God decided that Gideon's army was too large to fight the Midianites; therefore, God told Gideon to release some men to return home. One of the ways God chose which men were to remain in the army and which were to leave was by how they drank water at the river. Some men fell to their knees and began drinking as much as they could. Their faces were directly sloshed into the cool, wet liquid. Other soldiers bent down and drank from *"cupped hands"* (V.6). Those who dropped to their knees and slurped the water with their faces downward were released from the rank of God's men.

We know that God was not just making a silly random test; God was purposefully examining the strength of each man. We know God was selecting warriors who exuded strength because God had previously sent 2,200 men home due to their being fearful. But the men who were drinking on their knees were not sent home due to fear; they were sent home due to lack of *focus*. How could they be alert to fight when they had their faces in the water? Their minds were more focused on the water than the war. The water appealed to them more because it was soothing to their physical bodies. It is definitely easier to choose to do things that feel comfortable to us. That's *why* it's tempting not to fight for righteous thoughts; it's easy to feel like we don't have to battle as long as no one can see if we are losing or winning. However, a city on the hill is seen because it's lit up from the inside. You want to be a warrior who is lit up from the inside of your mind.

God wasn't pleased with the warriors who weren't prepared for action. Preparing for action starts in the thought life. 1 Peter 1:13 says, *"Therefore, prepare your minds for action; be self-controlled; set your hope fully on the grace to be given you when Jesus Christ is revealed. As obedient children, do not conform to the evil desires you had when you lived in ignorance."* You must train yourself to keep your mind set on the promises of God. Don't let worry, fear, or negative thoughts sink into your mind. You are a warrior! It's your privilege to put up a fight for the things you let reside in your mind.

The first time I went on an international mission trip, I was seventeen years old. I remember practically having a mental panic attack. I thought about all the horrible things that could happen. I wasn't controlling my thoughts at all! I also experienced those feelings of hesitations when I knew God was calling me to talk to someone at home about the gospel message. The reason why I got so discombobulated was because I wasn't keeping my thoughts on truth, light, and life; essentially, I wasn't fixing my gaze on Jesus and his desires for my life.

The war for holiness takes place in your reflections. Your mind is a chamber full of secrets, hidden paths, memories, dreams, and even temptations. The thoughts you allow yourself to dwell on can be dangerous. What if you were as careful with your thoughts as you were with a loaded gun? Each thought is like a bullet, and the gun is the mind; you purchase your bullets, and then decide where you want to aim. If you choose to have loving thoughts, then you choose bullets that will pierce the darkness. But choosing thoughts that are cruel, rude, or impure will surely become a homicide to the Light. The darkness knows that your thoughts are powerful, and that's why there are so many temptations to think ungodly, impure, and selfish thoughts.

Part of choosing pure thoughts is what putting on the helmet of salvation means. The helmet has been used throughout the centuries during all types of warfare. Symbolically, the helmet is what guards the head, and inside the head resides the thoughts of mankind. But salvation is something that is a choice to receive: *"Therefore, my dear friends, as you have always obeyed—not only in my presence, but now much more in my absence—continue to work out your salvation with fear and trembling"* (Philippians 2:12). This verse can seem confusing; how are you supposed to work out your salvation, if human works don't bring salvation? Wasn't salvation a gift? Of course it was a gift, but the Bible also says that faith without the accompaniment of actions is useless. God expects that if you believe something you will live it out.

When Moses and the Israelites were fleeing from slavery in Egypt, they encountered a block in the road: it was the Red Sea. God had already promised deliverance to the Israelites, so God wasn't pleased when they were standing around complaining. The Israelites were more focused on the massive sea that lay before them than the faithful promises of God. Exodus 14:15 says, *"Then the LORD said to Moses, 'Why are you crying out to me? Tell the Israelites to move on."* I love this verse! God is basically saying, "Good grief! I've given you feet! Just move it!" God operates like this in regard to your thought life, as well. You have been empowered by God to deal with your thoughts.

When I worked for a department store, my manager would say, "I'm empowering you to take care of a situation." That goes along with what God wants to say to us: "I've given you the ability to say yes or no to a thought." Unfortunately, minds tend to wander. Whether our thoughts are formed around idolatry, adultery, selfish ambitions, a worried heart, or lack of trust, if you know that your thoughts are not of God, then you have been given the power to say exactly what Jesus said to Satan: " *'Get behind me, Satan! You are a stumbling block to me; you do not have in mind the things of God, but the things of men. '"* (Matthew 16:23).

I encourage you to learn the skill of "thought blocking." It's a powerful way to defeat unwelcome contemplations. You can train yourself to quickly block unholy thoughts by switching directions. As you continue to practice this shifting of thoughts, you will experience greater victory in your reflections. It's your privilege, as a warrior, to dispel thoughts you know are not of God.

God's desire for us as his people is to keep our thoughts fixed on him. Paul also was concerned about the thought life of believers: *"But I am afraid that just as Eve was deceived by the serpent's cunning, your minds may somehow be led astray from your sincere and pure devotion to Christ"* (2 Corinthians 11:3). There is a promise about being controlled in your thought life; what does Romans 8:6 tell you are attributes of having clean thoughts? _____.

Remember that the Lord has given you the authority to stop your mind from thinking improper, unholy, and burdensome thoughts! Ask God to search your heart like Jeremiah did: *"Yet you know me, LORD; you see me and test my thoughts about you. Drag them off like sheep to be butchered! Set them apart for the day of slaughter!"* (Jeremiah 12:3).

Application:

What do you think God thinks about?

_____

_____

_____

_____

_____

_____

_____

_____

_____

_____

What has been on your mind the most lately? Is it glorifying to God? What thoughts do you find yourself struggling with?

_____

_____

_____

_____

_____

_____

Is there a certain situation you get into which causes you to be like that in your thought life?

_____

_____

_____

_____

_____

_____

How do your thoughts affect the battle of living for God?

_____

_____

_____

_____

_____

_____

_____

_____

_____

What steps can you take to begin controlling your thoughts today? How can you be more careful with that "loaded gun" you carry?

_____

_____

_____

_____

_____

_____

In the seventh and eighth centuries B.C. the Assyrian armies had helmets which included "hinged earpieces."[2] How is it symbolic that they were protecting the ears by protecting the head? How will guarding what you hear help you in your thought life?

_____

_____

_____

_____

_____

_____

There are other activities that affect your thought life. What activities do you think affect you most? (Example: music, TV, movies…)

_____

_____

_____

_____

_____

_____

Continue to ask the Lord for direction in your thoughts. Ask him to help you battle against ungodly thinking. He will assist you. Remember that he wants you to be victorious!

Verse to Remember: *Finally, brothers and sisters, whatever is true, whatever is noble, whatever is right, whatever is pure, whatever is lovely, whatever is admirable—if anything is excellent or praiseworthy—think about such things* (Philippians 4:8).

Quote to Consider: No matter where you go or what you do, you live your entire life within the confines of your head. –Terry Josephson[3]

Now, I implore you as a soldier of Jesus Christ, fight *the good fight...finish the race...keep the faith* (2 Timothy 4:7).

Day 10

Dissension in the Rank

Theme: Exuding Tolerance

You, my brothers, were called to be free. But do not use your freedom to indulge the sinful nature; rather, serve one another in love. The entire law is summed up in a single command: "Love your neighbor as yourself." If you keep on biting and devouring each other, watch out or you will be destroyed by each other.

Galatians 5: 13-15

Tolerance is *key* when dealing with new acquaintances. We are human; it doesn't take a lot to make us irritable. Patience is a fruit of the Spirit, but fruit takes a while to develop. It's important to note that if fruit is not properly maintained it will quickly rot. For me, working on the mission field was one of the greatest awakenings to who I actually was. You've probably met a lot of interesting people; maybe you've even had some unpleasant encounters with a few of them.

God knew that there would be problems between humans; he anticipated arguments, disagreements, and even wars. Yet, he *still* called you to reach the nations alongside of other people. Jesus picked twelve men to follow him, and he sent them out two by two. Despite his knowledge of typical conflicts between humans, he knew that we would be better if we had each other. *"Two are better than one, because they have a good return for their labor"* (Ecclesiastes 4:9).

But, honestly—don't people just get on your nerves? There are personality conflicts, idea disagreements, and clashing habits that are overwhelmingly irritating. People are obsessively negative, obnoxiously positive, overly smiley, not smiley enough, tenaciously lethargic, nauseatingly hyper, frustratingly unresponsive, and ridiculously talkative. It's mind-blowing! You get what I'm saying; sometimes we just don't mesh well with other people. But it doesn't matter what reason you have for disliking someone; you were called to love them regardless of their strange quirks. You were called to be patient with them, to care about their well being, and to want the best for them *despite* your differences.

Your brothers and sisters in Christ are your fellow warriors for the *cause* of Christ. You battle together! You take on the enemy of your souls together. You need to be tolerant of them. Don't stab them with the equipment God gave you for battle. Those weapons were meant to be sharpened against theirs for training: *"As iron sharpens iron, so one person sharpens another"* (Proverbs 27:17).

In Exodus 17, a fight takes place between the Israelites, the nation of God, and the Amalekites, a brutal, war-like people. In this chapter, Moses holds up his arms in order to receive the victory. As long as his arms were raised, the Israelites were triumphant. But Moses couldn't maintain strength in his arms for the entire battle. Read what happens: *"As long as Moses held up his hands, the Israelites were winning, but whenever he lowered his hands, the Amalekites were winning. When Moses' hands grew tired, they took a stone and put it under him and he sat on it. Aaron and Hur held his hands up—one on one side, one on the other—so that his hands remained steady till sunset. So Joshua overcame the Amalekite army with the sword"* (V.11- 13).

Aaron and Hur came to the rescue of Moses by their willingness to help their leader. In order for the battle to be successful, every warrior had to be strong for the next. Romans 15:1 says, *"We who are strong ought to bear with the failings of the weak and not to please ourselves."* Could you imagine if Aaron glanced at Hur, during the battle, and said, "Hur, my mom said you were a bad warrior..."? Wait, that sounds silly; no one would argue during such a calamitous situation. Yet, as a matter of fact, they do... *we* do. We point out each other's flaws; we cast blame, point fingers, and form opinions that generate hate.

You, my friends, are in extreme circumstances everyday. You are fighting for a world that is lost. The people who are far from God aren't ignorant; just because someone doesn't know Jesus doesn't mean they are totally oblivious to how you treat each other. They see your body language, your eye movements, and attitudes. It's sad to think that the destruction caused in the body of Christ can come straight from *ourselves*. *"What causes fights and quarrels among you? Don't they come from your desires that battle within you?"* (James 4:1). Remember that you are a warrior *all* the time. You are God's man, God's woman; you are in his uniform.

Let the battle bond you with your comrades. You have a common enemy, so why aren't you close to each other?! When one of you is weak, the other can be strong. Arguments are about pride. Don't be fixated on the flaws of your fellow warrior. *"Do not repay anyone evil for evil. Be careful to do what is right in the eyes of everybody. If it is possible, as far as it depends on you, live at peace with everyone"* (Romans 12:17 -18*). "As far as it depends on you"* means that *you* are responsible for the way you handle a situation. Joel 2: 7- 8 also discourages the purposeful act of provoking others. In this passage, Joel mirrors the way horses charge forward to the way we should advance: *"They charge like warriors; they scale walls like soldiers. They all march in line, not swerving from their course. They do not jostle each other; each marches straight ahead. They plunge through defenses without breaking ranks."* I like the word *"jostle"* used in this verse; jostle in the dictionary means to "bump, push, shove, brush against, or elbow roughly or rudely."[1] You might not literally shove someone, but words can be exceedingly brutal sometimes. If you witnessed the impact of your words, I bet you'd see a lot of bruises. Mean comments break spiritual arms; and the catch is… those are *your* arms too. Everyone is each other's— your hands, your feet, your mind, your mouth doesn't just belong to you. You are the body of Christ, and if the body chops up other members, the ability to operate in truth, life and peace will eventually be annihilated.

"The body is a unit, though it is made up of many parts; and though all its parts are many, they form one body, so it is with Christ...If the whole body were an eye, where would the sense of hearing be? If the whole body were an ear, where would the sense of smell be? But in fact God has arranged the parts in the body, every one of them, just as he wanted them to be. If they were all one part, where would the body be? As it is, there are many parts, but one body. The eye cannot say to the hand, 'I don't need you!' And the head cannot say to the feet, 'I don't need you!' ...If one part suffers, every part suffers with it; if one part is honored, every part rejoices

with it." (1 Corinthians 12:12-26).

Application:

Are there some co-warriors you are having a hard time getting along with? If so, do you think you had a preconceived notion or prejudice about that person before the mishap? Ask God to reveal your heart to you.

What are your thoughts and feelings about them currently?

_____

_____

_____

_____

_____

_____

_____

_____

How does it make you feel knowing that your attitude toward them affects the cause of Christ?

_____

_____

_____

_____

_____

_____

_____

Here are some tips on how to mend a difficult relationship.

- Remember to pray for each other. If someone is aggravating you, then pray for them. Ask God to correct the areas of their life where you see them struggling. Satan wants to rob your fellow warriors of good relationships. Ask God to give you a compassionate heart for them. Remember that blessing them is also a blessing to yourself; as they develop, they will be able to be strong when *you* are weak.

- Don't be afraid to speak with them. The Bible says to first personally confront your brother or sister in Christ (Matthew 18:15). If they still won't be cordial, then ask someone of authority to speak to them with you a second time.
- If you choose to approach the situation, bear in mind to use words of encouragement. Think about qualities they possess that are good; focus on those. Communicate to them the strengths you notice in them; kind words go a long way." *A gentle answer turns away wrath, but a harsh word stirs up anger"* (Proverbs 15:1).

Verse to Remember: *Blessed are the peacemakers, for they will be called sons of God* (Matthew 5:9).

Quote to Consider: If we have no peace, it is because we have forgotten that we belong to each other. – Mother Teresa[2]

Now, I implore you as a soldier of Jesus Christ, fight *the good fight...finish the race...keep the faith* (2 Timothy 4:7).

Day 11

Life Breather

Theme: Spreading Encouragement

as long as I have life within me, the breath of God in my nostrils,

Job 27: 3

He was led to a valley—a valley where dead men's bones lay. Being led by God, Ezekiel walked *"back and forth among them"* (Ezekiel 37:2). God then said "... *'Prophesy to these bones and say to them, "Dry bones, hear the word of the LORD! This is what the Sovereign LORD says to these bones: I will make breath enter you, and you will come to life"* (V.4-5). As Ezekiel obeyed God's instructions, he watched the bones fuse together and heard their *"rattling sound"* (V.7). Even though all the bones were connected, there was no life in them. So the Lord commanded Ezekiel to speak breath into the *"slain, that they may live"* (V.9). As Ezekiel prophesied, *"breath entered them; they came to life and stood up on their feet—a vast army"* (V. 10).

Words are powerful. By Ezekiel's act of obedience to be a speaker of life, an entire valley of bones was reattached. Ezekiel ushered from the dead *"a vast army"* (V.10). There is another army that is on the move, and you're in it; it's the army of God. Like Ezekiel, you've been appointed to raise up an army of *spiritually* dead men to join your revived rank. The Bible constantly addresses the intense influence of the spoken word (Proverbs 6:2; 16:24;

Ecclesiastes 5:2). The power of God's words spoken and breathed out to other people is physically evident. Jesus displayed that power when he called to life several people, including a little girl in Mark 5:41: Jesus, "...*took her by the hand and said to her, 'Talitha koum!' (which means 'Little girl, I say to you, get up!').*" He also called forth his dear friend, Lazarus, from the grave in John 11:43. And if that's not enough to awaken our understanding of the influence of words, then look at the ground, your fingers, and at nature—they were also spoken to life by God (Genesis 1).

It's important to not just see the physical things that Jesus did through his words. It's much more crucial to observe that he brought dead men and woman back to a *holy* life. The physical realm is purely a mirror of what God wants to do in the spiritual realm. Jesus desires that all men not only come to know him, but that they thrive spiritually. You can be a part of the advancement that causes people's souls to flourish.

Unfortunately, talking *can* be used as a tool of the enemy. Sometimes it is hard to see the impact of words. But nonetheless, the effects of lies are deadly. When bodies start disintegrating, they ooze an unpleasant odor. In the same way, there is a literal aroma of the spiritual realm. Spiritually dying people smell like coarse joking, slander, mean comments, and curse words (Romans 1:29). However, you aren't dead. You're alive! (Colossians 2:13). Therefore, I encourage you to use speech that reveals *life*.

It's easy to slip and utter things that you don't always mean or shouldn't say. It's easy to make passing comments, small remarks, and whispered insults that you think nobody notices. However, I assure you, if are you speaking death someone is listening, and someone is dying. Words that produce death destroy the work of the Lord. It's heartbreaking to consider that the language of God's people could actually harm his righteous cause. "*With the tongue we praise our Lord and Father, and with it we curse men, who have been made in God's likeness*" (James 3:9).We must do whatever we can to get rid of spiritual bad breath.

When you are breathing encouragement into people, you reverse the spiritual death process. It's like CPR for the soul. Your words can be an instrument of healing (Proverbs 12:18). You can pump life into someone's spiritual body! Keep in mind that you might have to breathe life into someone for a while before they start to breathe on their own. You might have to persist in telling someone that God loves them before they even flinch like they are coming to life. But continue to spread life through your speech!

Your words can touch someone and help to push back the forces of the enemy in their lives. When the soldiers came to arrest Jesus, all the soldiers literally fell over when Jesus spoke. John 18:6 says, *"When Jesus said, 'I am he,' they drew back and fell to the ground."* In the same sense, you can speak with such power that Satan must retreat.

Besides speaking life into those who don't know God, it's important to speak encouragement to fellow warriors as well. In Isaiah 41:6, unrighteous soldiers were encouraging each other in their evil ways: *"they help each other and say to their companions, 'Be strong!'"* If evil encourages its members, then how much more should you encourage your co-warriors in Christ?

Each day you have a choice; will you choose to be an instrument of life? Be determined to love others through God's words of encouragement today. Use as many sincere and authentic compliments as you can! Make today a compliment day by spreading love, truth, and life through the words you speak. Be a life breather. Be faithful to be the air of heaven—the army is waiting to *live*.

Application:

Can you remember the most meaningful compliment ever given to you? What was it?

_____

_____

_____

_____

_____

How did that affect your life, your morale, your self-image?

_____

_____

_____

_____

_____

Just as you benefited from encouragement, ask God to bring people to mind whom you can encourage today. God may ask you to speak to certain people, and it might not make sense to you. But remember that God lead Ezekiel to the dry bones, and God will be faithful to lead you to those who need encouragement. List some people here that God brings to mind. Possibly jot down a scripture you can give them that will fill their spirit man.

-
-
-
-

As you go throughout the day, ask God to continue revealing more people that may need to be encouraged. Lastly, remember to be sensitive about the words you use. Be guided by the Holy Spirit. While everyone benefits from encouragement, not everyone comes from the same background. Their tolerance of words may be different from yours. So make sure you get your purpose across.

Verse to Remember: *"The words of the wicked lie in wait for blood, but the speech of the upright rescues them."* Proverbs 12:6

Quote to Consider: How wonderful it is that nobody need wait a single moment before starting to improve the world. –Anne Frank[1]

Now, I implore you as a soldier of Jesus Christ, fight *the good fight...finish the race...keep the faith* (2 Timothy 4:7)

Day 12

Inevitable Persecution

Theme: Suffering with a Smile

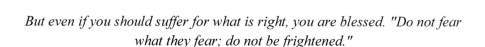

But even if you should suffer for what is right, you are blessed. "Do not fear what they fear; do not be frightened."

1 Peter 3:14

Jesus made a promise about persecution; the promise wasn't that you would bypass it, but that you would endure it everywhere you went. Expecting people who don't know Jesus to love you is an unrealistic, unbiblical idea. The world won't love you. The world won't appreciate your trying to reach them for a God they don't believe in or a God they may have bitter feelings toward. Harassment, hatred, and hostility should be expected; that's part of what it means to carry your cross (Matthew 10:38). You are not exempt from trials because you are a part of God's people. On the contrary, you are immersed into trials *because* you are a part of his family, his army, and ultimately his life. You aren't going to glide through life without having someone hate you. It's a part of the call. God foreknew that you would walk through hard times because of your dedication to him. He knew that people would call you names, spit at you, turn on you, laugh at you, curse you, shun you, push you, run from you, and mock you. You're going to have people tell lies about you, point at you, steal from you, report you to the authorities, tell you that you're crazy, and even demand that you leave.

The central difficulty isn't dealing with people who persecute you.

The major struggle is controlling *yourself*— your response to those people. You might want to push them, hate them, hit them, scream at them, and tell them they're insane. But you can't alter their actions; you can only direct your own response. You were born to fight *for* them, not *with* them.

The Apostle Paul endured several extreme experiences because of his faith. Look up 2 Corinthians 11: 24-28, and list some of the troubles he encountered:

-

-

-

-

-

-

-

Even after all Paul suffered, he was still filled with zeal for godly living. What does he instruct you to do in James 1:2-3? And what reason does he give for it?

_____

_____

_____

_____

As you realize the inevitability of suffering, it's easy to feel defeated. But the Bible encourages you to delight in your suffering. God doesn't necessarily desire that you go through horrendous circumstances; he hates to see his children in pain! However, he knew that humanity was sinful and that evil would not hold back from causing you trouble. Still, God's plans are beautiful because he has created the journey of suffering to become a *blessing*. God does not want your mind to be absorbed in suffering; he desires that you be fixated on joy. "…*Do not grieve, for the joy of the LORD is your strength*'" (Nehemiah 8:10).

There are reasons to rejoice in the midst of persecution. Suffering with a smile doesn't mean you won't feel the pain; it means that you get past the ache and see the lovely outcome. The first joyful aspect of suffering is that it reveals true living. If the darkness couldn't see the light in you, they wouldn't feel the need to persecute you. If you have been careful to preach with love, and you're still opposed, that means you're doing something *right*. It means that you are walking in the truth. You are the target of evil's contempt. The darkness abhors you! You are exactly what Satan is fearing— you're a God-loving, Jesus-serving fanatic who won't settle for anything less than loving the lost to the Lord!

Light, life, and truth are all wrapped up in one person— "*Jesus answered, 'I am the way and the truth and the life. No one comes to the Father except through me*" (John 14:6). Part of winning the battle is remembering that Satan detests the light in you, and he will hate you via other people. The darkness in them hates the light in you, the death in them hates the life in you, and the lies in them hate the truth in you. But it's a reason to rejoice that the darkness knows who you are. The darkness can see God in you. You are the "*light of the world*" (Matthew 5:14)! What an honor!

Suffering also serves as a magnetic mechanism for fusing you to Jesus. It's a uniting tool between you and God. Knowing that you are suffering for Christ means that you must be walking close to him. Part of the beauty of belonging to God is that you can experience what he experienced, which will ultimately bond you to him. The world of sin may despise you, but essentially they are helping you understand what it means to be Christ. Their disapproval strengthens your friendship with Jesus! "'*If the world hates you, keep in mind that it hated me first*" (John 15:18). You're not merely suffering for him, you're suffering *with* him. Paul said, "*I want to know Christ—yes, to know the power of his resurrection and participation in his sufferings, becoming like him in his death,*" (Philippians 3:10).

A third blessing that comes from suffering is the anticipation of future reward. "*This is what the LORD says: 'Restrain your voice from weeping and your eyes from tears, for your work will be rewarded,' declares the LORD…*" (Jeremiah 31:16). The Bible says that Jesus was able to endure the cross because there was something wonderful set before him (Hebrews 12:2). While suffering, Jesus looked forward to seeing us with him in heaven. There is joy set before you as well: you receive the blessings of God in your everyday life (James 5:11). You pour into other people's lives, and you inherit eternal life! Even if you only see a small portion of goodness on earth, you can look forward to eternity. *"I consider that our present sufferings are not worth comparing with the glory that will be revealed in us"* (Romans 8:18). *"Therefore we do not lose heart. Though outwardly we are wasting away, yet inwardly we are being renewed day by day. For our light and momentary troubles are achieving for us an eternal glory that far outweighs them all"* (2 Corinthians 4:16-17). *"Blessed is the one who perseveres under trial because, having stood the test, that person will receive the crown of life that the Lord has promised to those who love him"* (James 1:12).

Application:

Have you recently experienced persecution for being like Jesus or being willing to evangelize? Maybe you feel like you are undergoing persecution simply by being away from your comfort zone. If it's not current, can you remember a time when you walked through trials for the cause of Christ?

_____

_____

_____

_____

_____

_____

_____

_____

How does what you're going through currently or what you've been through change your perspective on what Christ went through?

_____

_____

_____

_____

_____

_____

_____

_____

We discussed three joys of persecution: being seen as the light, connecting closer to Jesus' trials, and getting to be rewarded. Which of the three joys mentioned applies most to your life, and why?

_____

_____

_____

_____

_____

_____

_____

If you aren't going through any persecution right now, is there anyone in your life whom you've seen suffer for the cause of Christ? What was their response? How did that make you grow, change, awaken in your spiritual walk?

_____

_____

_____

_____

_____

_____

_____

_____

_____

_____

_____

V**erse to** R**emember**: *We are hard pressed on every side, but not crushed; perplexed, but not in despair; persecuted, but not abandoned; struck down, but not destroyed. We always carry around in our body the death of Jesus, so that the life of Jesus may also be revealed in our body. For we who are alive are always being given over to death for Jesus' sake, so that his life may be revealed in our mortal body* (2 Corinthians 4:8-11).

Q**uote to** C**onsider:** To endure the cross is not tragedy; it is the suffering which is the fruit of an exclusive allegiance to Jesus Christ. –Dietrich Bonhoeffer[1]

Now, I implore you as a soldier of Jesus Christ, fight *the good fight...finish the race...*keep *the faith* (2 Timothy 4:7).

Day 13

Worship Warrior

Theme: Devastating Satan's Plans through Praise

The LORD is my strength and my shield; my heart trusts in him, and he helps me. My heart leaps for joy, and with my song I praise him.

Psalm 28:7

They stepped out first: trekking with purpose, marching with faith, singing with praise into battle. They were the first to be seen and heard by the enemy. The weapon they were fighting with was more powerful than man-made metals. They were treading into war with a *thankful* heart.

It was early in the morning. They were headed for the Tekoa Desert, when Jehoshaphat gave his warriors a word from the Lord: " *'Listen to me, Judah and people of Jerusalem! Have faith in the LORD your God and you will be upheld; have faith in his prophets and you will be successful.' After consulting the people, Jehoshaphat appointed men to sing to the LORD and to praise him for the splendor of his holiness as they went out at the head of the army, saying: 'Give thanks to the LORD, for his love endures forever'"* (2 Chronicles 20:20-21). Can you imagine what it would feel like to be the one chosen to sing praises at the head of the army? Despite the tempting human response to run in the face of the enemy, they stayed and, *"As they began to sing and praise, the LORD set ambushes against the men of Ammon and Moab and Mount Seir who were invading Judah, and they were defeated"* (2 Chronicles 20:22).

The nation of Judah was saved from overwhelming defeat because they walked forth with a song of praise on their lips. Praise ushers in victory because it strips Satan of all authority, honor, and reward. It also reveals certainty in the fanatic faithfulness of God. Having a heart of worship is imperative because it crushes Satan's attempts to destroy your faith, your certainty, and your trust. When you're going out onto the field, it's vital to carry an attitude of worship. The worshippers in Jehoshaphat's army were armed with thanksgiving. For people of God, praise is an expectation because it stems from the realization of God's abilities and accomplishments. *"Sing joyfully to the LORD, you righteous; it is fitting for the upright to praise him"* (Psalm 33:1).

Worship that comes through faith cannot only serve to glorify God and strengthen you, but it also serves as a method of ministry. Part of living the God-life is setting spiritual captives free who are imprisoned in darkness (sin). Isaiah 61:1 says, *"The Spirit of the Sovereign LORD is on me, because the LORD has anointed me to proclaim good news to the poor. He has sent me to bind up the brokenhearted, to proclaim freedom for the captives and release from darkness for the prisoners,"* It's not simply a good idea to battle for those who are in the midnight of evil; it is a calling to combat for them. You must recognize that going forth with God's praise on your lips is powerful.

Paul and Silas experienced the influence of praise while they were chained in prison. *"About midnight Paul and Silas were praying and singing hymns to God, and the other prisoners were listening to them. Suddenly there was such a violent earthquake that the foundations of the prison were shaken. At once all the prison doors flew open, and everyone's chains came loose"* (Acts 16: 25-26). What a remarkable moment that must have been—seeing physically what was happening spiritually! While God wants to break physical strongholds in the lives of people, he also wants to break spiritual strongholds. Praise is one method of escorting in spiritual freedom. The Scriptures say, *"everyone's chains came loose."* It wasn't only Paul and Silas who were set free—all the prisoners were freed. In essence, your praise is a magnet for lost souls.

People were meant to know truth and receive the Spirit of the Lord.

The Word of God says, "*God is spirit, and his worshipers must worship in the Spirit and in truth*'" (John 4:24). It was vital that Paul and Silas sing aloud because "*...the other prisoners were listening to them...*" (V.25). Other people hear everything you say, even if you think they're not listening. Part of being a praise bearer is letting people know the One who can break their chains (Colossians 3:16). Since Paul and Silas were singing aloud, the prisoners knew that Paul and Silas were asking the Lord of Lords for his help and thanking him for his faithfulness. Therefore, once the prisoners were set free, they knew who to praise for their freedom.

Sometimes fanatic, emphatic worship is scary because we wonder what those around us think. We fear that we may be shunned. But in 2 Samuel 6, David unashamedly took off his royal outerwear and danced in his ephod (robe). When Saul's daughter, Michal, saw David in the street, she insulted him and told him that the slave girls would spurn him. But David said something noteworthy about the girls who saw him praising— "*But by these slave girls you spoke of, I will be held in honor'* " (V.22). David realized that praising God is beautiful, not disgraceful. David committed to— *become even more undignified* (V.22) if that's what it would take to wholly praise God.

I'm not telling you to boogie in a foreign boulevard. However, I do encourage you to vulnerably reveal your praise. Strip off the clothes of insecurities, and extol God with all your might! Hopefully, you will get a chance to hear some worship music today. Worship God as extremely as possible (whatever that means for you). Maybe you need to jump, kneel, or sit. It's between you and God. But commit yourself to being someone filled with the edification of God's work. Whenever you're speaking praise, someone's life will be changed! Remember that praise is also reflected in your attitude, facial expressions, tone, and body language. Ask God to help you be a temple of total praise! Remember that the army of Judah sent out their praise first. Send out your worship of God first thing today. Remember, praise proceeds victory. Being armed with thanksgiving will serve to devastate Satan's plans, set captives free, and ultimately give God glory.

Application:

Take this time to write a letter to God. Tell God how wonderful he has been in your life. Praise him for what he's done, doing, and going to do!

How do you see that your praise will help you in fighting spiritual battles?

_____

_____

_____

_____

_____

_____

_____

_____

Activity: Tell somebody the praise that you have. Tell them who God has been to you. As you move out to reach people for the Kingdom, let the praises of God go before you. Ask God to make the praise on your lips evident to those around you. For with that powerful praise, their chains will fall off!

Can you think of a song you can hum in your spare time that will be your march of praise? _____.

Verse to Remember: *Because your love is better than life, my lips will glorify you. I will praise you as long as I live, and in your name I will lift up my hands. I will be fully satisfied as with the richest of foods; with singing lips my mouth will praise you* (Psalm 63:3-5).

Quote to Consider: Praise now is one of the great duties of the redeemed. It will be their employment for ever— Albert Barnes [1]

Now, I implore you as a soldier of Jesus Christ, fight *the good fight...finish the race...*keep *the faith* (2 Timothy 4:7).

Day 14

The Solo Soldier

Theme: When God hides his Face

We are given no signs from God; no prophets are left, and none of us knows how long this will be.

Psalm 74:9

He didn't understand what it meant to be born again. Nicodemus had a hard time grasping why he would have to return to infanthood when he was already a grown man (John 3). He didn't realize that he would need to grow up spiritually just like he grew up physically. When Jesus instructed Nicodemus of his need to be reborn, he wasn't speaking to Nicodemus alone; Jesus meant that all of us must be rebirthed into his likeness (1 Peter 1:23). When we came into Christ, we entered in as newborn babies. Part of growing spiritually is gaining eyes to see.

When babies are first born, their visual perception is not well developed. They are only able to view objects that are eight to twelve inches from their face. Over the course of being a newborn until four months old, they obtain the ability to view depth. During that time, their capability to distinguish the light from the dark is also formed.[1] However, due to babies' flawed eyesight, exercises such as peek-a-boo assist with quicker refinement of their vision.

Babies genuinely believe a person had disappeared when they play the game of peek-a-boo. The child's vision is not mature enough to realize that the person is still nearby.[2] Likewise, attaining visual spiritual maturity is recognizing that God's movements, whether seen or unseen, are not a reflection of his existence or his work in a matter. It's easy to feel like God disappears when we no longer see results. Although peek-a-boo is thought of as a game, God is using his seemingly hidden face as an exercise to enhance your spiritual sight. His purpose for your life is continued spiritual growth through which he will be glorified. Sometimes it's tempting to assume God has abandoned the scene when you can no longer feel him or hear him. Maybe you believe that God has disappeared from your life or from your missions work because you don't see situations or people changing. But he hasn't left. God is merely exercising your *vision* of him.

I struggle the most to feel God's nearness when I'm out of my ordinary surroundings. When I lived in Büsingen, Germany for a while, it was difficult for me to sense the presence of God. It wasn't because I lacked the company of amazing people; it was simply because it's easier for me to feel the Lord's closeness when I'm in my normal surroundings. Maybe you feel that way, too. Maybe you've been away from your "God place" for a while, and therefore sense he's no longer near. But God wants you to remember that he is omnipresent. One of his names is "*...Immanuel' (which means 'God with us')* (Matthew 1:23). He is bound to his name. It is his contract.

God is near to his people. You have not been abandoned, deserted, or forgotten by God. Maybe you feel alone, misunderstood, and ultimately disregarded. However, God doesn't leave you. People may flee, but the Lord never will. You can stand on this: your journey through life is not marched alone; God endures with you. He doesn't fall asleep on the job. Your Commander has not left you; he is *training* you. You are not a solo soldier. God wants your vision of him to improve, and therefore he may hide himself. The more he appears and "disappears," the more frustrated your spiritual eyes become. Eventually that frustration will give way to new depth of sight. Just as small babies increase their ability to view dark from light, your spiritual eyes will be better able to distinguish the spiritual light from the spiritual dark as you grow. Don't halt quality time with your Savior because you don't feel him.1 John 2:28 says, "*And now, dear children, continue in him, so that when he appears we may be confident and unashamed before him at his coming.*"

In the New Testament, Jesus said that he does not label us as servants, but he calls us friends (John 15:15). He is the friend who will never leave. *"One who has unreliable friends soon comes to ruin, but there is a friend who sticks closer than a brother"* (Proverbs 18:24). God does stick close. He is a reliable, dependable, unfailing friend.

Consider this: if God were distant and only occasionally attentive, then he would have not commanded you to *"pray continually,"* (1 Thessalonians 5:17). The very fact that God instructs you to call on him unceasingly states that he is there *all* the time to listen. You aren't unaided because you can't see God. His footprints will be seen through your character building. Psalm 77:19 says, *"Your path led through the sea, your way through the mighty water, though your footprints were not seen."*

Part of dealing with the feeling of God's absence is calling yourself to remember his faithful presence. Between Psalm 42 and 43, the Sons of Korah say identical lines three times: *"Why, my soul, are you downcast? Why so disturbed within me? Put your hope in God, for I will yet praise him, my Savior and my God"* (Psalm 42: 5, 11; Psalm 43:5). Moses also informed the people of the Lord that they needed to carefully watch their hearts' thoughts about God's closeness. *"You saw no form of any kind the day the LORD spoke to you at Horeb out of the fire. Therefore watch yourselves very carefully,"* (Deuteronomy 4:15). The reason behind Moses' warning was so that the people would not be tempted to create *"... an idol, an image of any shape..."* (V.16).

It's your choice if you let the ability or inability to see God's appearance strengthen you or squash you. Satan wants you to surrender to the belief that you are undoubtedly alone. If you choose to believe that lie, then your faith will begin to disintegrate. Satan purposes to tempt you into idolatry. He wants you to put a person, a circumstance, or an activity in the place of God. The Lord, on the other hand, wants you to remain fixated on him. He has purposed the seasons of peek-a-boo as an exercise to make you strong.

Whether you feel the presence of God or not, remember that he doesn't clock out for break. When you turn over in your sheets tonight, he's guarding you. When you laugh, he's smiling. When you cry, he's holding you. When you speak to him, he's listening—despite your vision of his nearness. God is a zealous lover and a best friend. Maybe you feel like God is hiding his face. In spite of these feelings, you must continue to believe that he is still there loving and caring for you. He is close. Use this time to grow.

"What other nation is so great as to have their gods near them the way the LORD our God is near us whenever we pray to him?" (Deuteronomy 4:7).

Application:

Can you remember a time when you felt far away from God? Maybe it's now. Either way, what are you going through, and how does it make you feel to know that he merely wants to strengthen your faith?

_____

_____

_____

_____

_____

_____

_____

_____

_____

_____

_____

_____

_____

_____

_____

Take a good look at yourself. Have you been faithful during the time of his "disappearance"? How?

_____

_____

_____

_____

_____

_____

_____

_____

_____

_____

_____

If not, in what ways can you commit to seek him more?

_____

_____

_____

_____

_____

_____

_____

What do you think God wants you to know today? What do you sense he is speaking to you?

_____

_____

_____

_____

_____

_____

_____

_____

_____

If you are going through a season where you can't hear him, spend some extra time in his Word.

Verse to Remember: *Yet I am always with you; you hold me by my right hand. You guide me with your counsel, and afterward you will take me into glory.* (Psalm 73:23-24).

Quote to Consider: He is with us on our journeys. He is there when we are home. He sits with us at our table. He knows about funerals and weddings and commencements and hospitals and jails and unemployment and labor and laughter and rest and tears. He knows because He is with us - He comes to us again and again - until we can say, It's You! It's You! –Bob Benson[3]

Now, I implore you as a soldier of Jesus Christ, fight *the good fight...finish the race...*keep *the faith* (2 Timothy 4:7).

Day 15

Taking the Highway

Theme: Living with Integrity and Excellence

Whatever you do, work at it with all your heart, as working for the Lord, not for human masters, Colossians 3:23

When the Roman warriors went onto the battle field, they were more than prepared for the conquest that lay before them. Legions upon legions of warriors were exceedingly qualified for combat. Each day they encountered rigorous training: "Every month they had to make three eighteen-mile marches. These had to be covered in a day while carrying sixty pounds of equipment, plus armor and weapons. They had to learn drill, which was both practice for movements used in battle and ceremonial performance. And of course they learned how to handle weapons..."[1] They understood that they needed to be exceptionally excellent, progressively paramount, and continually competent if they were going to war.

It's hard to maintain excellence when we are tired, frustrated, or simply not in the mood. However, if the Roman soldiers were not prepared to fight, they could potentially lose their lives when it came time to practice mimicking the "schools for gladiators."[1] In the same way, as people of God, we need to be skilled. We need to be excellent braves for the cause of Jesus Christ. If we aren't ready to be admirable in everything we do, then we lose not only our self-respect, but ultimately we can lose the authenticity of our testimony.

The armies of the Romans were *known* for their way of fighting, and they were recognized for being outstanding in battle. In the same way, the reputation you build for yourself reflects what others will think of God. It's important to question your work; are you are performing tasks in a manner that will cause people to recognize you as a Christian? By declaring the name of Jesus Christ, you are embracing the duty to be a person of excellence. But if you don't serve whole-heartedly, how will a needy world know that there is a God who whole-heartedly strives for them? How will they see that there is a God who loves them and rules them with justice and integrity? Leviticus 19:2 says, "*'Speak to the entire assembly of Israel and say to them: "Be holy because I, the LORD your God, am holy."*"

Being holy is what it means to walk upon the way that is superior: "*And a highway will be there; it will be called the Way of Holiness; it will be for those who walk on that Way. The unclean will not journey on it; wicked fools will not go about on it*" (Isaiah 35:8).When you accepted God into your life, you enlisted yourself into his total, undefiled character. When you decided to live in the purity of truth, then you chose to live in an admirable manner. You wear his Name. All your actions say something about Jesus. That's a great honor and a grave responsibility.

In order to effectively *declare* the good news, one must first *embody* the good news. If you don't subsist in excellence, integrity, and holiness, then you don't live to the standard of the gospel. Jesus is the highest bar of integrity. Everything Jesus accomplished was done with all his might. He walked with a fervor and zeal that was more than merely emotional. He strode with selflessness, truth, and love. He accomplished excellence by means of living with undefiled character. Jesus didn't cut corners or accomplish tasks halfway. He walked on the "*highway.*"

If Jesus had conceded to living complacently, then he might have *habitually* not finished the task on the cross. He may have remained there for only a few minutes. Now, that wouldn't have been beneficial! He had to *finish* in order to *save* us. He had to complete. He had to do it right, do it well. He crammed his massively holy self into a minute, sinful world. He lived here unselfishly. He resolved to give his life in entirety. Isn't that what you and I are called to? We are called to live our lives just like the One who saved our lives. Holiness and excellence may be the easiest concepts to preach, yet the hardest principles to live. However, attitudes produce actions. Hence, the importance of obtaining a John 3:30 attitude, "*He must become greater; I must become less.*" If we walk forward armed with the desire to make *God* visible through our lives, then eventually excellence will merge into all facets of our daily activities.

I've experienced temptation to slack off at work, at home, and even on the mission field. The more people around, the easier it was to pawn off work. But God revealed to me that even if others weren't aware of my lack of work, he didn't miss a thing. God sees *everything*. Maybe it's easy to slack off sometimes because we forget that God is attentive to our lives. However, the scriptures proclaim that God rewards and punishes us according to our actions (Proverbs 3:33).

Not being an excellent individual affects the entire Body of Christ. Complacency is *contagious*. If you've ever set up Christmas lights, you can vouch for how frustrating it is when you have one broken bulb; it causes all the other bulbs to no longer shine. Likewise, if one member of the Body of Christ is slacking off, then others may choose to do the same. You are a leader, like it or not. Someone will eventually follow in your footsteps. Ask yourself what trails you are making for others to follow.

Don't waste your time on the mission field. You will have ultimate joy when you are seriously devoted to the cause of Christ. Remember, mediocrity contaminates. Patchy devotion isn't pleasing to God. He wants you to be *sold out*, completely committed, and fanatically excellent in every way!

Maybe there is something that you know you can perform better. Maybe there is a task that you've been given, and you are only doing it in a manner so as to not exhaust yourself. Remember that in *all you do*, you perform unto God! Wear yourself out for Christ! You are his name bearer, and when people see your good actions, they will turn and glorify God! *"Live such good lives among the pagans that, though they accuse you of doing wrong, they may see your good deeds and glorify God on the day he visits us"* (1 Peter 2:12).

Remember, bearing the name of Jesus is an honor. And Jesus proclaimed: "... *'Whoever wants to be my disciple must deny themselves and take up their cross and follow me"* (Mark 8:34).

Application:

Excellence is defined as "possessing outstanding quality or superior merit," and it also means to be "remarkably good."[2] How does your life reflect God, who is remarkably good?

_____

_____

_____

_____

_____

_____

_____

When do you find it most difficult to maintain excellent living? Is it in thought, word, or deed? Maybe it's at a specific place such as work, home, school, or the mission field?

_____

_____

_____

_____

_____

_____

What movements can you make today toward becoming a more excellent individual?

_____

_____

_____

_____

_____

_____

Verse to Remember: *Those who have served well gain an excellent standing and great assurance in their faith in Christ Jesus* (1 Timothy 3:13).

Quote to Consider: The world never burned a casual Christian at the stake. – John R. Rice[3]

Now, I implore you as a soldier of Jesus Christ, fight *the good fight...finish the race...*keep *the faith* (2 Timothy 4:7).

Day 16

Something Beautiful

Theme: The noninstantaneous miracles

But as for me, I watch in hope for the LORD, I wait for God my Savior; my God will hear me.

Micah 7:7

He pulls into a fast food drive through. His mouth is dripping with hunger. His eyes are fixed on the menu. He quickly places his order. But through the small speaker, he hears a voice proclaim the unthinkable, "Sir, it will be a couple extra minutes; the chicken isn't quite ready."

The man's inner, hungry monster comes out; he throws his hands up, "What do I have to do to get a meal around here?!" he exclaims.

If you're smirking right now, it's probably because that's something you've done. You've been upset over not getting your chicken nuggets quickly enough. But, in reality, you'd probably willingly wait a few minutes rather than be contaminated with salmonella. Waiting can be a healthy, good, life-saving concept. One of the major upsets of humanity is that we want things immediately—at the very second we say "mine!" We put a product called "Miracle Growth" on our lawns. We upgrade our internets every couple of months. We don't even want to wait on coffee to brew. The words "waiting" and "miracle" don't seem to connect. I agree that it sounds like an odd mixture of words. One might ask oneself, "How can waiting be a miracle"? Unfortunately, the hasty attitude used in ordinary life circumstances is also reflected in our spiritual walk.

We often neglect the fact that God doesn't fulfill the desire for rush; he completes the desire for right. He is more involved with performing the *correct* outcome in *perfect* timing, than dashing to the cause of human satisfaction. Besides, who said things were better if they were quicker? It seems that we humans want the most luxurious, comfortable situation, but we aren't willing to wait for it. It's rare to see someone who is thrilled about having to wait. Nobody I know jumps up and down and shouts, "Goody, nothing's happening!" Sadly, we want God to be like a fun-sized genie who sits on our shoulders and bestows our every wish. If he answers us immediately, we say he's miraculous, and if he does not, we say that he's not moving. But just because God isn't moving *instantaneously*, doesn't mean that he isn't moving *miraculously*. The lack of *obvious* response does not mean the lack of powerful shifting. The need for instant miracles revolves around our human yearning to be satisfied. We believe that things will only be beautiful if they're done our way right away.

Our human longing for immediate results creeps into the way we do ministry as well. It's difficult to feel productive when you share the message of the gospel with someone who isn't quick to respond. Living in the midst of seemingly unresponsive people is frustrating. Nine times out of ten, you won't see someone instantly drop to their knees in repentance. However, God promised that he would do his part to draw them. Romans 2:4 says, "...*God's kindness is intended to lead you to repentance...*" The term "*lead*" in the Greek is ἄγω (ag'-o) which means to "bring to the point of destination."[1] When one is bringing something, it is in a process. In the same way, bringing people to the point of their destination in Christ is most often not an instantaneous event. Even if a person was miraculously healed by your laying on of hands, they may never tell you.

I was in Peru in 2003, serving as a short-term missionary. One evening, we missionaries were exiting the bus to perform a skit for a church service. I was appointed to make sure everyone was off the bus. But I noticed Lisa, one of the other missionaries, remaining in the very last seat. She held her stomach and informed me that she was extremely ill. I helped her to her feet, placed my hands on her, and I asked God to heal her completely. She said a quick "thanks" and walked with me to the church. Later during the trip, everyone was asked about two of their favorite memories. When it came time for Lisa to describe her favorite memory, she looked over at me and said that it was when I laid hands on her to pray. She described the feeling of God sweeping over her body and healing her instantaneously. She expressed that the presence of God spread through her, and she had "never experienced anything like it." I sat there shocked; I had no clue that she had been healed!

Sometimes people won't tell you what God has done in them. You may pray over someone, and they might not tell you if God has moved. There are several reasons. First, humans tend to have their guard up. We don't want others to always know what we are experiencing. Secondly, it may be pride. The leap from darkness to light is a huge step; if someone has walked in darkness for a long time, they may pretend to hold their ground. Thirdly, they may not be convinced of their healing. They may feel good for a moment, but they may be unsure if the healing will remain.

Birthing something in the spiritual realm that is lasting, full grown, and ready for life is a mirror to what takes place in the physical realm. For nine months, you were turning, growing, and forming into a fully developed baby. As humans, we expect that it will take a while for a baby to be brought into the world. Yet we don't share that same glorious patience when it comes to spiritual birthing. It's easy to let what our physical eyes see determine reality. But since when did you use your physical ears and eyes to do all your sensing? "*He has made everything beautiful in its time. He has also set eternity in the human heart; yet no one can fathom what God has done from beginning to end*" (Ecclesiastes 3:11).

Remember that whether your prayers are answered immediately or not, God is working. He might not move all at once, but he is in the process of making something beautiful.

Application:

Can you remember a time when you thought God wasn't moving, only to find out later that he really had?

_____

_____

_____

_____

_____

_____

_____

_____

_____

_____

_____

Is there a current situation in your life where you feel like God isn't moving?

_____

_____

_____

_____

_____

_____

_____

How does it make you feel knowing that God is working, even when he doesn't appear to be?

_____

_____

_____

_____

_____

_____

_____

What do you think God wants you to realize today about his movements?

_____

_____

_____

_____

_____

_____

_____

_____

Continue to lay hands on, speak truth to, and love everyone. God is working; hand him your total trust.

Verse to Remember: *Let us not become weary in doing good, for at the proper time we will reap a harvest if we do not give up* (Ephesians 6:9).

Quote to Consider: Cast not away your confidence because God defers his performances. That which does not come in your time, will be hastened in his time, which is always the more convenient season... -- Matthew Henry[2]

Now, I implore you as a soldier of Jesus Christ, fight *the good fight...finish the race...*keep *the faith* (2 Timothy 4:7).

Day 17

The Letter Shredder

Theme: Casting Out the Lies

I crushed them completely, and they could not rise; they fell beneath my feet. You armed me with strength for battle; you humbled my adversaries before me. You made my enemies turn their backs in flight, and I destroyed my foes.

2 Samuel 22:39-41

Satan gives you fail mail. If you had a spiritual mailbox, he would send you hundreds of letters a day. He jots down insults for you, hoping that you will take heed and ultimately believe them. He writes you negative memos purposed for your destruction. His messages are coded and dripping with hatred. He desires to ruin your knowledge of your identity in Christ and bring annihilation to the cause of Christ. But Satan knows that the only way he can try to maul the revolution of Christ is by clawing *you*. You are God's hands and feet! Satan notices God in you, and bearing God's light is an irreplaceable honor! But that reputation causes restlessness in your refuter, and he becomes an intruder who joyously takes on the role of your accuser. However, your refuter, intruder, and accuser is a *liar*.

Satan is the father of deceit, discouragement, and distress "*...He was a murderer from the beginning, not holding to the truth, for there is no truth in him. When he lies, he speaks his native language, for he is a liar and the father of lies*" (John 8:44). Even though you don't call him "*father*," he will try to speak into your life as if he were. He puts on facades to look radiant.

He even masquerades his letters so you won't know who sent them. He wants them to look like they are written by God, when they aren't. Unfortunately, Satan is passionate about his job, and he's good at it. He's been doing it for a long time. He knows how to get you upset, ruffled, and disheartened. He is quick to birth hesitations and fears about going and reaching people for Christ because he is afraid of you. He is afraid of freedom. He is afraid of light, truth, and love. But part of using the weapon of wisdom is recognizing your human inclination to feel inadequate, self-conscious, and timid. Satan will use your weak tendencies as *strategies*.

There are two common states of emotion that every human encounters: the feelings of inferiority and insecurity. Inferiority is when we experience "feeling lower in position, stature, or value."[1] Insecurity is when we suffer from "the state of not being secure, not confident, not firm."[2] We are prone to being crushed because we don't remember how vital it is to have a correct view of ourselves. However, it's *imperative* to see ourselves the way God sees us. It's easy to disregard the importance of self-care. However, self-destruction that is birthed from lies will only reap devastation. Displaced self image will affect your spiritual walk and your ministry. If your life is going to be fully lived for the King, then you must have an accurate, Biblical view of yourself.

Studying the Bible in its original written language is eye opening. One of my favorite Greek words used in Scripture is ὑπερνικάω (hoop-er-nik-ah'-o).[3] This word alone sums up the phrase "more than a conqueror" found in Romans 8:37, which states, *No, in all these things we are more than conquerors through him who loved us.* The word ὑπερ (hoop-er) means to be over or above, and νικάω (nik-ah'-o) is the word for conqueror.[4] How much higher can you get than being *above* someone who is victorious?

You really are higher than Satan. Romans 16:20 states that the Lord would, "*...soon crush Satan under your feet...*" The word for crush in the Greek is συντρίβω {soon-tree'-bo} which literally means to "break, to break in pieces, shiver, to tread down, to put Satan under foot and (as a conqueror) trample on him, to break down, crush, to tear one's body and shatter one's strength." [5] How amazing is it that because you carry the life of God within your body you are literally "breaking" Satan "in pieces" (2 Corinthians 4:10)! You crush Satan with your very existence! And he hates that, so he turns and tries to crush you. But never worry, you win this minute by minute crush because "*... You, dear children, are from God and have overcome them, because the one who is in you is greater than the one who is in the* *world"* (I John 4:4).

The cruel words of the darkness are futile because they are false. You live God's life out, and there is nothing feeble about the life of God. Your imperfections do not categorize you as a failure. How can you not succeed when you are in step with the One who is utterly perfect?

Satan doesn't want you to know what power you have in your life. He doesn't want you to know that God calls you a *"special possession"* (1 Peter 2:9), or that Jesus said you could perform *"even greater things"* than he did (John 14:12). But you don't have to worry about those masked letters from Satan. Even if you read them or hear them, God has given you steps to becoming a letter shredder. Maybe you've even received the same letter for years. Maybe every day you wake up feeling not good enough, attractive enough, strong enough, smart enough...The list goes on and on of human insecurities. However, you can overcome the lies that Satan has planted in your heart. Your life doesn't have to be trampled by the thoughts Satan has about your heart, your call, or your personhood. In Christ, you can overpower the enemy. There are three steps to crushing the influence of Satan's words over your life: resist, rebuke, and recite...

- Resist the acknowledgment of Satan's lie.
- Rebuke him for his advances.
- Recite scripture to make him flee.

Some people say that you should never talk to the Devil. But Jesus never told you not to talk to the Devil; he told you not to *believe* the Devil. You can't rebuke him without communicating with him. He talks to you all the time. There's nothing wrong with rebuking Satan. Talking to him won't kill you, *befriending* him and *believing* him will. Command Satan to get away from you, but tell him to leave with scripture. He throws letters at you, but you can throw the letters of God (Scripture) back at him. It's vital for you to replace the pocket of space where you cast the lie out with the truth. Remember that the darkness is exempt from the light. You can say to Satan, "Get away from me; I am *more than* a conqueror *through him* who loves me (Romans 8:37), and I will trample you under my feet!" Take a look; it's exactly what Jesus did in Matthew 4: 8-11: *Again, the devil took him to a very high mountain and showed him all the kingdoms of the world and their splendor. "All this I will give you," he said, "if you will bow down and worship me." Jesus said to him, "Away from me, Satan! For it is written:*

'Worship the Lord your God, and serve him only.'" Then the devil left him, and angels came and attended him.

Remember, you have been armed with the strength of God; all his mighty power is at work in you (Colossians 1:29). You are a ὑπερνικάω (conquering) individual! And you can συντρίβω (crush) your enemy.

Application:

Spend some time in the spiritual trade hub; exchange lies you've taken into your belief system for truths found in Scripture. When you stand on the promise of being a conqueror, you can trade tears for joy, discouragement for excitement, worry for peace, brokenness for wholeness, and ultimately, failure for victory.

In what ways do you feel Satan attacks you the most? List some areas of struggle in your life:

_____

_____

_____

_____

_____

_____

_____

_____

_____

_____

_____

_____

_____

_____

_____

_____

What thoughts do you have about yourself that are clearly not from God?

_____

_____

_____

_____

_____

_____

_____

_____

_____

_____

_____

_____

_____

How do you notice those lies keeping you bound on a daily basis?

_____

_____

_____

_____

_____

_____

_____

_____

_____

_____

_____

Once you have pinpointed specific lies that Satan tries to mail to you, shred those lies by finding scripture that will bring truth to your heart.

Here is a sample for you to practice rebuking the enemy with scripture:

I, _____, will not be a part of your plans, Satan. In the name of Jesus Christ, I command you to flee from my presence. The lies you've been telling me, _____ , is false. The Bible says that I am *fearfully and wonderfully made* (Psalm 139:14), that I am a *conqueror* (Romans 8:37), and that *I can do all* things through Christ *who gives me strength* (Philippians 4:13).

I love to think about how symbolic it was that, even at the beginning of time, God cursed the snake by making it crawl on its belly (Genesis 3:14). God took away the feet and legs of the snake! Symbolically, God disarmed Satan's authority to walk on us. But he gave us spiritual feet! And then, through the power of the cross, he armed us with his power so that we could crush Satan.

Sometimes the best way to remember a concept is by making it a physical reality in our lives. My charge for you today is to literally write the name of Satan on the bottom of your shoes. That way with every step you take you can constantly and consciously be stomping on the enemy of your soul! If you don't want to literally write his name, then I encourage you to write the verse reference, Romans 16:20.

Verse to Remember: *Where, O death, is your victory? Where, O death, is your sting?"* (1 Corinthians 15:55)

Quote to Consider: "I often laugh at Satan, and there is nothing that makes him so angry as when I attack him to his face, and tell him that through God I am more than a match for him" – Martin Luther[6]

Now, I implore you as a soldier of Jesus Christ, fight *the good fight...finish the race...*keep *the faith* (2 Timothy 4:7).

Day 18

Rock Solid Arms

Theme: When Storms Won't Relent

You answer us with awesome and righteous deeds, God our Savior, the hope of all the ends of the earth and of the farthest seas,

Psalm 65:5

When God called you, he purposed that you would be a fisher of mankind (Matthew 4:19). Being a fisherman means that you're on the water… constantly. Likewise, you are daily on a sea of temperamental waters, and there are dangers that come with fishing. Fishermen will tell you that the worst upset is a raging storm in the middle of their quest. The second most frightening sight is nearby rocks that could crush their boat. Storms don't hold back their ferocity simply because one is fishing. Similarly, when life's mishaps occur, sometimes they are uncontrollable dilemmas.

Life is full of struggles. Period. Calamity can rock you back and forth to the extent of literally feeling nauseous. Unfortunately, signing up in the army of God never gave anyone a holy exemption against dealing with life. There are still fender benders, financial blindsides, and a variety of unfortunate run-ins. But you are called to be a warrior even during the seasons of hurricanes. However God does not leave you in the storm with no hope and no equipment. God gave you a tool called an anchor.

No one knows for sure when anchors were invented. Some claim it was the Greek philosopher, Eupalamus, who invented the first anchor.[1] Yet no matter where they originated, they have been immensely helpful to sailors throughout history. In fact, over the course of time, ships were designed with multiple anchors. In Acts 27, Paul encountered a storm on the Adriatic Sea. They *"dropped four anchors from the stern"* in order to hold fast (V. 29). In the same way, you are created with four anchors that help you remain steady during unexpected and difficult situations. Your four anchors are your heart, soul, mind, and strength (Mark 12:30). Anchoring these areas of your life is accomplished by anchoring your focus on the Lord. Despite the scary squalls and stormy situations at hand, you can still keep your gaze fixed on God and channel all your energy into seeking him.

Your heart anchor means focusing on God with all your might and vigor. Your soul anchor is your determination to keep your spiritual life intact. Your mind anchor is fastening your thoughts on God. And your strength anchor is your physical self being obedient to his commands. It is true that anchors are supposed to keep one from drifting. Yet real anchors don't always hold. The theory that you will be saved by dropping your anchor of focus on God is flawed. Seeking God will save you in the sense that you are able to get your eyes off your circumstance, but it doesn't always save you from the storm itself. Storms don't relent simply because your eyes are on Jesus. We know this from Matthew's account of Peter walking on the water (Mathew 14). When Peter miraculously walked on water, his eyes were locked on Jesus. But when he took his eyes off Jesus, he was filled with fear from the sight of the fierce wind. His eyes had been on Jesus, but the storm didn't depart.

It was probably terrifying for Peter to see the wind and waves crashing around. Peter, being a fisherman (Matthew 4:18), understood the dangers that could occur with terrible sea weather. And Peter was also literally *in* the waves. Maybe you feel like you are in the waves. Maybe you fear dreadful situations. Unfortunately, horrible circumstances can occur even when you're focusing on God. So what if you hit those rocks that line your seas? Then what? Then you must realize that God calls himself the rock. *"The LORD lives! Praise be to my Rock! Exalted be God my Savior!"* (Psalm 18:46). You may wonder how that can be. How can you dash against a rock and run into God at the same time? My friend, God catches you in the midst of your circumstance. He's there. He lines your stormy seas, and he has rock solid arms that are love. You might bump into troubles, but predicaments don't triumph; they can serve to push you into God. The irony is that when you think you are being dashed against the rocks of life, you are really being dashed into the Rock who *is* life—he is the Lord Almighty. Don't you know he pulls you close to him in your pain? Jesus said, *"Blessed are those who mourn, for they will be comforted"* (Matthew 5:4). God is sovereign. Keep in mind that no matter what the enemy means for your destruction, no matter how many rocks you feel yourself dashing against, no matter how much you sway and tumble, you will bump right into God. He is the rock called salvation. He is everywhere around you. *"You hem me in behind and before, and you lay your hand upon me"* (Psalm 139:5).

There was a time where I wore an anchor chain around my neck every day. I purposefully wore it to symbolize my anchor of focus being on God. Even though I was overwhelmingly determined that my anchor would hold fast, it still was the hardest time I've ever encountered. I have never cried so hard, been so broken, or experienced so much pain. I had never encountered such outrageous storms! I was in the midst of spiritual hurricanes. Yet I had to remind myself that I will always dash into God, even if life is painful.

Remember to drop your anchors of focus on God even if you are crashing into a rock right now, and even if you can feel pain all around you. God called you to focus on *him* despite the reality of hitting the rocks. Life's unpleasant moments happen. Yet you are called to center yourself on God. Get your eyes off your circumstance, Warrior. Don't worry about the possible pain; there are rock solid arms to hold you.

Application:

Remember that letting your anchor down is obedience. You have four anchors: heart, soul, mind, and strength. Is there a specific anchor you know you haven't dropped? Which one? How do you think you can work on focusing your heart, soul, mind, or strength on God?

_____

_____

_____

_____

_____

_____

_____

_____

_____

_____

What are some raging storms you've been dealing with?

_____

_____

_____

_____

_____

_____

_____

_____

_____

_____

Do you feel like you're bumping into rocks? What does it mean to you to know that God calls himself the rock? What does that tell you about his sovereignty?

_____

_____

_____

_____

_____

_____

_____

_____

_____

_____

Verse to **R**emember: *He is the Rock, his works are perfect, and all his ways are just. A faithful God who does no wrong, upright and just is he* (Deuteronomy 32:4).

Quote to **C**onsider: If we cannot believe God when circumstances seem be against us, we do not believe Him at all. –Charles H Spurgeon.[2]

Now, I implore you as a soldier of Jesus Christ, fight *the good fight...finish the race...*keep *the faith* (2 Timothy 4:7).

Day 19

The Sweetest Words

Theme: Revamping the Heart

"Come now, let us settle the matter," says the LORD. "Though your sins are like scarlet, they shall be as white as snow; though they are red as crimson, they shall be like wool.

Isaiah 1:18

There is a type of sadness that is precious to God. It's a blessed distress, a consecrated concern. It's humanity being distraught over their sin. Without a holy sorrow, there would be no repentance. *"Godly sorrow brings repentance that leads to salvation and leaves no regret, but worldly sorrow brings death."* (2 Corinthians 7:10). It's especially tempting when one is in an evangelistic status to become more focused on how everyone else is living their lives. But the Lord wants us to daily check our own hearts. Jesus said , *"You hypocrite, first take the plank out of your own eye, and then you will see clearly to remove the speck from your brother's eye"* (Matthew 7:5).

Unconfessed and unacknowledged sin can be damaging to our ministry. It blocks our insight into other's lives, which keeps us from helping them grow in purity of heart. Matthew 7:5 says we can *"clearly"* see the struggles in others if we first deal with our own internal issues. The Bible also teaches that sin leads to death (James 1: 14-16), and it's hard to be a living vessel if you're filled with the aroma of death. The people you minister to will recognize your life, light, and love for God. It is displayed through your actions. It's scary to think about, but the amount of sin in your life is a measuring tool for the love you have for God; this isn't a man-made concept. *"Jesus replied, 'Anyone who loves me will obey my teaching. My Father will love them, and we will come to them and make our home with them"* (John 14:23).

When we belong to God, the actions that break his heart will break our hearts as well. The desire to merge into God's likeness yields us to fanatical Godly living. *"See what this godly sorrow has produced in you: what earnestness, what eagerness to clear yourselves, what indignation, what alarm, what longing, what concern, what readiness to see justice done..."* (2 Corinthians 7:11). How amazing to have *"earnestness," "eagerness," "indignation," "alarm," "longing," "concern,"* and *"readiness"* to let go of sin! When someone chooses wrong doings, essentially they are burying the armor they use for spiritual warfare; their sword, breastplate, helmet, belt, ready feet, and shield are all thrown down.

Marvelously, there is something God created in order for you to get your armor back—repentance. Confession is like telling God where you buried the righteousness he entrusted to you. Then he goes to the places you hid your weapons. He kneels down in the dirt and digs them up for you. You couldn't have found them on your own. You had to watch your Commander get down in the slum and unbury the gifts he gave to you. You had to watch him struggle and put his own body down into the ground, in order to find what it was you lost. In the most symbolic way, he placed his body in the ground and died there, so that he could resurrect not only his life but your clean heart. Isn't it wonderful that he never holds against you the fact that he helped you, loved you, and died for you?

Satan hates your God-given authority to say "no" to sin. He doesn't want you to be aware of what you're doing. He will try to block your spiritual eyes from recognizing right and wrong. He's after you at all costs. Satan wants to keep you locked down and powerless. He would rather you cover up your faults than take them to Jesus. He will make your stored sin glazed over with white. Remember, he masquerades as light, and he also disguises sin to look appealing and fun or nonexistent. He suggests that you ignore your transgressions.

However, sin keeps you from God, whether you acknowledge its presence or not. Even if a person doesn't understand they are sinning, it doesn't mean the effect, cost, and consequence of sin are lessened. God said that, due to lack of understanding, his people will not survive: *"my people are destroyed from lack of knowledge...*" (Hosea 4:6). Continued repentance is a part of spiritual survival.

In the Old Testament, burnt offerings were necessary in order to receive forgiveness from God. Christ had not come yet to be the ultimate sacrifice for the world. Sin was such a serious dilemma between God and mankind that they had to offer sacrifices for even unknown sins. The seriousness of sin has not changed. The unrelenting striving to be like God is still very present; it's an every-moment decision.

I walked through a season of guilt due to unacknowledged sin. In a way, I felt like God wouldn't want to pardon me because I had failed multiple times. But as I lay in bed one evening, the Holy Spirit spoke straight to my heart; as loud and as soft as a whisper, he said: "*If we confess our sins, he is faithful and just and will forgive us our sins and purify us from all unrighteousness*" (1 John 1:9*). Those are the sweetest words.

God is heartbroken over sin because of what sin does to you. Sin kills (Romans 6:16). If you respond casually to sin, you'll become a casualty of sin. God desires that you be alive and free—totally emancipated from the consuming clutch of death. "*It is for freedom that Christ has set us free...*" (Galatians 5:1) Freedom is attained through obedience, and part of being subservient is maintaining a heart of confession. It's hard to admit wrong doings. But it's much better to walk without the shame that feels like shackles.

Consider how much God loves you. God also hates sin because it pulls you away from him. All God wants to do is hold you. But sin pushes his arms away. Choosing to ignore righteousness is like putting God behind your back. Graciously, God doesn't treat humanity the same way. He doesn't put *you* behind his back; he puts "*sin*" behind his back. "*Surely it was for my benefit that I suffered such anguish. In your love you kept me from the pit of destruction; you have put all my sins behind your back.*" (Isaiah 38:17).

Remember that God's grace was never meant to be twisted into an excuse for more sin. That kind of thinking is straight from the enemy. "*Live as free people, but do not use your freedom as a cover-up for evil...*" (1 Peter 2:16).

Remember also that approaching Jesus for forgiveness is only available today; tomorrow isn't promised. Take advantage of your time. Keep in mind that the payment for your freedom was expensive. You were bought with blood—the only medicine that could save you. "*Jesus said to them, 'I tell you the truth, unless you eat the flesh of the Son of Man and drink his blood, you have no life in you*" (John 6:53). It's tragic that the Lover of our souls had to die for us. But it's radically reviving to know that he would want to clean us up, even if it cost his life.

Application:

Proverbs 20:5 says, "*The purposes of a person's heart are deep waters, but one who has insight draws them out.*" Ask God for insight of any hidden way in you. I encourage you to do a heart check. Ask the Great Physician to check your spiritual heartbeat.

What sins do you have stored up in your heart that you need to deal with? Are there any specific sin(s) you feel God is showing you?

_____

_____

_____

_____

_____

_____

_____

_____

_____

_____

_____

_____

Is there a place, state of mind, or even certain days when you find it's easiest to fall into the trap of sin?

_____

_____

_____

_____

_____

_____

_____

_____

_____

_____

_____

What steps can you take to avoid giving into temptation? If you're not sure what to do, ask God to help you recognize an escape route from sin. He'll always provide a way out for you (1 Corinthians 10:13).

_____

_____

_____

_____

_____

_____

_____

_____

Christ accomplished the demolition of your sin on the cross. But is there something that stands in the way of you sincerely confessing, repenting, and changing?

_____

_____

_____

_____

_____

_____

_____

_____

_____

The weight of sin can be carried around for so long that it's tempting to forget it's even there. Maybe you keep putting a certain subject on the back burner with God because you don't want to tell him. Remember that *"The LORD is compassionate and gracious, slow to anger, abounding in love"* (Psalm 103:8).

> # Verse to Remember: *I am writing to you, dear children, because your sins have been forgiven on account of his name* (1 John 2:12).
>
> # Quote to Consider: Sin and the child of God are incompatible. They may occasionally meet; they cannot live together in harmony --John R. W. Stott[1]

Now, I implore you as a soldier of Jesus Christ, fight *the good fight...finish the race...*keep *the faith* (2 Timothy 4:7).

The Phenomenal Exchange

Theme: Needing His Name

Some trust in chariots and some in horses, but we trust in the name of the LORD our God.

Psalm 20:7

How horrifying it must have been for mothers and fathers to drop their dead babies at the base of an idol, so that their idol god would "feel" worshipped. That is how it was for many pagan nations in the Old Testament. They were required to present their idol with whatever gift might persuade it to perform its duties. [1] Therefore, when they wanted to serve the fertility god, they were required to give their children as a sacrifice. It was an outrageous ritual; how sickening that they felt they needed to bribe their god into action. However, it's eye-opening for us because we can see with clearer eyes how gracious and good our true God is to us.

We can point fingers at those who endeavored to entice their gods. We can call them crazy and shun their ways. We may even feel tempted to shake our heads at their foolishness because they were so blinded to their bizarre beliefs of beguiling their god into action. But, in reality, sometimes we try to make promises to God based on our wanting of him to reveal himself. We say things like, "If he only would heal us, then we would… If he would speak and show up, then we would…. If he would spare us this one time, then we would…" But God doesn't want us to feel like we must persuade him to be true to his name. His name is free! God doesn't make us give to him what he is to us; he doesn't expect us to exchange strength for strength or knowledge for knowledge. No, we trade our faults and follies for his forgiveness and faithfulness.

It's easy to forget how frequently we need to run to God and how *freely* we can run to him. Unanticipated, painful situations normally cause us to throw ourselves into the arms of people around us. While it is good for us to have companions on the journey, God wants his name to be our initial and enduring companion. He wants his name to be what we reach for first! He is jealous for us! Exodus 34:14 says *"Do not worship any other god, for the LORD, whose name is Jealous, is a jealous God."* God wants his name to be our remedy—what our minds cling to, what our faith holds to, what we whisper in the night, what we sing in the shower, what we scribble in our notebooks, what we long for, and what we live for.

Calling on God is a part of activating your romance with him and your faith in him. In the Bible, God changed several people's names according to what they would accomplish in the future. It was a statement of expectation in what would come to pass. For example, the name of Abram was altered to Abraham, meaning "lofty father." (2 Kings 23:34; 24:17; 1 Samuel 25:25). The name Jacob changed into Israel (Genesis 17:5) and Simon, son of John, became the name of Peter, which means "rock" (John 1:42).

Not only were changing names seen as a source of prophecy or fulfillment over someone's life in ancient times, but they also could be given to someone *after* an event took place. For example, the name Isaac meant "laughter," which is how his mother expressed herself when she received the promise of Isaac's birth (Genesis 18:12; 21:6). In the same way, God's name serves as a prophecy of not only who he is going to be for us, but what he has already been. As his people, it's our duty to acknowledgement his Kingship and authority in our lives. In Leviticus 22:32 God said, *"Do not profane my holy name, for I must be acknowledged as holy by the Israelites…"*

Sometimes there is simply nothing else one can do except call on the name of the Lord. Marvelously, the Bible consists of 625 names for God!

That's more than the days found in a year, hours in a day, minutes in an hour, and seconds in a minute. How symbolic that God's name is more than enough for each passing moment; he has more attributes to save us than we have moments in a lifetime!

Besides the benefit of the ability to beckon God at every moment, using God's name will also be profitable for ministry. Matthew 12:21 says that, "*In his name the nations will put their hope.*'" Declaring the name of the Lord as your saving mechanism will assist you in bringing truth to the nations. God's desire is that, as we make him our primary helper, the people who are around us will see his work in our lives and will desire to take the name of the Lord as their salvation.

I don't know what situations you're encountering currently. I don't know what you dreamed about last night or what you thought about this morning. I have no idea if you've been dropping tears on your pillow or if you've been beaming with delight. Maybe you just need to be rescued from a situation, a mindset, or possibly feelings you have toward a person—God knows, and he promised he would liberate, love, and be loyal to you. Everyone's experiences are unique to what God is trying to teach them. Fortunately, when all of us come to the Lord, he is enough for each one of us! He is enough for you! He is enough for me!

Remember that there are no magic spells, no perfect bribes, no potion or cream that can soothe or bring power to a situation. God alone is our saving: "*Our help is in the name of the LORD, the Maker of heaven and earth*" (Psalm 124:8). "*No one is like you, LORD; you are great, and your name is mighty in power*" (Jeremiah 10:6).

Application:

Circle, underline, or highlight which names you need God to be for you today. Read through the entire list. God might want to be something for you that you didn't even realize you need.

Song of Solomon 1:3, "*Pleasing is the fragrance of your perfumes; your name is like perfume poured out...*"

Abba (daddy) Rom 8:15

Above All Eph 4:6

Almighty God Deut 10:17

Alpha & Omega Rev 21:6

Always Awake Ps 121:4

Amen, The Rev 3:14

Avenger Ps 94:1

Calmer of Storms Ps 107:29

Clothed With Strength Ps 93:1

Comforter Is 66:13

Compassionate Lam 3:22

Conqueror of My Enemies Ps 108:13

Consolation Rom 15:5

Consuming Fire Deut 4:24

Counselor Is 28:29

Covenant Keeper Ps 89:34

Creator of the North & South Ps 89:12

Defense Ps 94:22

Deliverer Ps 91:3

Director of My/Our Path Prov 3:6

Doer of Wonders Ps 77:14

Dwelling Place Ps 90:1

El Shaddai (God Almighty) Ex 6:3

Everlasting Arms Deut 33:27

Excellence Is 28:29

Faithful Lam 3:23

Father Is 63:16

Feeder of the Hungry Ps 146:7

First & Last Is 41:4

Forgiving Num 14:18

Fortress Ps 91:2

Gentle Is 40:11

Giver of Good Things Matt 7:11 Jms 1:17

Glorious Ps 76:4

Good Ps 145:7

Gracious Ps 145:8

Great Ps 145:3

Guide Ps 48:14

Habitation Ps 91:9

Healer Ex 15:26

Healer of Broken Hearts Ps 147:3

Helper Ps 146:5

Hiding Place Ps 32:7

High Tower Ps 144:2

Holy One Is 12:6

Holy Lev 19:2

Husband Is 54:5

Husbandman (Gardener) Jo 15:1

I Am Ex 3:14

Infinite

Understanding Ps 147:5

Jealous Ex 34:14

Jehovah Jireh (God will provide) Gen 22:14

Jehovah Nissi (God our banner) Ex 17:15

Jehovah Shalom (God our peace) Judges 6:24

Jehovah Shammah (God is there) Ez 48:35

Jehovah Tsidkenu (our righteousness) Jer 23:6

Judge Gen 18:25

Just Is 45:21

Keeper Ps 121:5

King of Glory Ps 24:10

King of All the Earth Ps 47:7

Lifter of Our/My Head Ps 3:3

Light Ps 27:1

Living Water Jer 2:13

Longsuffering Num 14:18

Lord Gen 15:2

Lord God Omnipotent Rev 19:6

Lord of Lords Deut 10:17

Lord of the Sabbath Ex 20:10
Lord on High Ps 93:4
Love 1Jo 4:8
Lovingkindness Ps 89:33
Majesty Ps 145:5
Maker of Heaven & Earth Ps 115:15
Man of War Ex 15:3
Merciful Eph 2:4
Mighty Lu 1:49
Mighty in Wisdom Job 36:5
Miracle Worker Matt 19:26
Most High Dan 7:27
Never Changing Jms 1:17
Near Ps 145:18
Never Weary Is 40:28

Omnipresent Ps 139:7 10
One Who Sanctifies Num 8:17
Peacemaker Prov 16:7
Physician Ps 103:3
Potter Is 64:8
Powerful Ps 66:7
Promise Keeper Is 46:11
Provider Matt 6:31
Ready to Forgive Ps 86:5
Reconciler 2Cor 5:18 19
Redeemer Is 54:5
Refiner Mal 3:3
Refuge Ps 46:1
Refuge from the Storm Is 25:4
Revenger Ps 94:1
Righteous Ps 5:8
Rock of Our/My Refuge Ps 94:22
Salvation Ps 91:16
Satisfier of Desires Ps 145:16
Saviour Ps 106:21
Shade on Our/My Right Hand Ps

121:5
Shadow from the Heat Is 25:4
Shepherd Ps 23
Shield Ps 3:3
Slow to Anger Ps 103:8
Song Is 12:2
Steadfast Dan 6:26
Strength to the Needy Is 25:4
Strength, Our/My Ps 46:1
Strong Ps 89:8
Sun, A Ps 84:11
Sustainer Ps 3:5
Teacher Ps 119
Trustworthy Ps 144:2
Truthful 1Sam 15:29
Upright Ps 25:8
Wise Dan 2:20
Worthy Rev 4:11[2]

Activity:

Isaiah 44:5 says, "*Some will say, 'I belong to the LORD'; others will call themselves by the name of Jacob; still others will write on their hand, 'The LORD's,' and will take the name Israel.*"

Now, you were probably taught at a young age not to doodle on your skin- but I encourage you to inscribe in your palm whichever name you need him to be for you today. Maybe you even want to do that daily. Jot it down on your hand as a reminder of who God promised to be for you, who he has already been, and what he has already accomplished. If you don't want to write it on your hand, put his name somewhere you will see it often. Let it serve to remind you that each moment you need to call on the name of the Lord he will be there! He will rescue you. He will delight in you. He will deliver you.

Verse to Remember: *The name of the LORD is a fortified tower; the righteous run to it and are safe* (Proverbs 18:10).

Quote to Consider: God is an unutterable sigh, planted in the depths of the soul. – Jean Paul Richter[3]

Now, I implore you as a soldier of Jesus Christ, fight *the good fight...finish the race...keep the faith* (2 Timothy 4:7).

Day 21

Weapons of Wisdom

Theme: Reaping Wisdom from Heaven

But where can wisdom be found? Where does understanding dwell?... It cannot be bought with the finest gold, nor can its price be weighed out in silver. It cannot be bought with the gold of Ophir, with precious onyx or lapis lazuli... Where then does wisdom come from? Where does understanding dwell?... God understands the way to it and he alone knows where it dwells, for he views the ends of the earth and sees everything under the heavens.

Job 28:12,15-16, 20, 23

Everyone receives wisdom from a source. People may gain insight from a friend, family member, or a counselor. However, if advice-givers aren't going to the scriptures, then there is wisdom that is missing—God's wisdom. God's opinion about a situation is immensely complex compared to our minute understanding. We can't conceive of all God's heavenly thoughts. *"As the heavens are higher than the earth, so are my ways higher than your ways and my thoughts than your thoughts"* (Isaiah 55:9).

The Bible teaches about the importance of obtaining the full armor of God for spiritual battles. Having wisdom will help you use the spiritual weapons correctly. Proverbs 24:6 says that wisdom is vital for fighting battles: *"Surely you need guidance to wage war, and victory is won through many advisers."* You are in a spiritual battle every day, not only for your own spiritual growth, but also for the souls who don't know Christ.

Therefore, obtaining wisdom from God is a key ingredient for victorious living and for effective evangelism. Ecclesiastes 9:18 states that, *"Wisdom is better than weapons of war..."* You are at war against the darkness. So, of course, the Holy Spirit will give you all the wisdom you need; he is on your side! He wants you to win the battles you wage!

Scripture says, *"...The Spirit searches all things, even the deep things of God. For who among men knows the thoughts of a man except the man's spirit within him? In the same way no one knows the thoughts of God except the Spirit of God. We have not received the spirit of the world but the Spirit who is from God, that we may understand what God has freely given us"* (1 Corinthians 2:10-12). God wanted to make a way for us to share in his ideas more readily. Therefore, God made his Spirit available to us. When Jesus left the earth, he gave the gift of the Spirit of God in order that we would be able to share in his thoughts.

In the same way that your biological relatives are a part of your genes, wisdom can be etched upon your heart and mind; it can be carried with you wherever you go. Ask God to help you be connected to wisdom this way. *" Say to wisdom, 'You are my sister,' and to insight, 'You are my relative'"* (Proverbs 7:4). What does this verse tell you about the closeness that is supposed to be between you and the thoughts of God?

_____

_____

What does Proverbs 8:12 say wisdom works along side of? And what are the attributes wisdom possesses?

_____

_____

Solomon, son of David, has been praised throughout history due to his admirable request to God. The Lord told Solomon that he could ask for anything and, *"Solomon answered God, 'You have shown great kindness to David my father and have made me king in his place. Now, LORD God, let your promise to my father David be confirmed, for you have made me king over a people who are as numerous as the dust of the earth. Give me wisdom and knowledge, that I may lead this people, for who is able to govern this great people of yours?'"* (2 Chronicles 1:8-10). It's true that Solomon's request was good. However, even though Solomon made a wise decision in his request, he didn't necessarily live out what he knew in his heart. Wisdom is easier to talk about than to walk out, for sure! Howard F. Vos describes some of Solomon's downfalls despite the wisdom God granted him: "…his (Solomon's) lack of fiscal judgment or fiscal restraint left the kingdom virtually bankrupt at his death. His lack of wisdom in marital matters resulted in the collection of a harem of seven hundred wives and three hundred concubines. This dramatically increased idolatry, the financial burden on the state, and created impossible conditions for the conduct of proper family life"[1]. Even though someone can have an abundance of wisdom it "does not necessarily mean that one will have the courage or restraint or perseverance to pursue a wise course of action."[1] When asking God for wisdom, make sure you commit yourself to following through with the wisdom being given to you.

Your life can be lived for the glory of God, and you can be victorious in all situations when you have his *mind*. God made a promise to you about wisdom and understanding. He doesn't want to hold it back from you; he is willing to pour it out like a monsoon over the thirsty lands of your life. Proverbs 2: 1-4 says, *"son, if you accept my words and store up my commands within you, turning your ear to wisdom and applying your heart to understanding—indeed, if you call out for insight and cry aloud for understanding, and if you look for it as for silver and search for it as for hidden treasure…"*

Read Proverbs 2:5; what does this verse say will happen?

_____

_____

_____

_____

And what does verse 8 say that he longs to do for you?

_____

_____

_____

Verses 9-11 are the results of what happens when you receive the thoughts that come directly from above: *"Then you will understand what is right and just and fair—every good path. For wisdom will enter your heart, and knowledge will be pleasant to your soul. Discretion will protect you, and understanding will guard you."*

Application:

Remember that James 1: 5 is a promise: *"If any of you lacks wisdom, you should ask God, who gives generously to all without finding fault, and it will be given to you."*

What do you need from the Lord today? What situation have you encountered where you could really use some of God's thoughts and wisdom? Tell him what wisdom you need from him:

_____

_____

_____

_____

_____

_____

_____

_____

_____

_____

_____

_____

_____

_____

_____

_____

_____

_____

_____

_____

Is the Holy Spirit bringing to your remembrance any specific words from Scripture that can help you in your situation?

_____

_____

_____

_____

_____

_____

Maybe you have already received the wisdom you need in a situation. Check your life; are you truly living out what you know to be wise? Ask God to show you what steps you can take today to be a wiser individual.

I encourage you to remain attentive to God's voice. He might speak through a situation, a sermon, or a worship song. You won't be forsaken in your request for wisdom because God wants you to have wisdom, understanding, and knowledge. He desires that you burn for his wisdom and seek it with your whole heart.

Ask someone today to war in prayer with you for wisdom. Then battle for someone else by asking God to give them his holy insight. I want to pray over you what the Lord said of Uri's son, Bezalel "… _I have filled him with the Spirit of God, with wisdom, with understanding, with knowledge and with all kinds of skills—_ " (Exodus 31:3).

Lord, I pray for wisdom, understanding, knowledge, and skill over those who are reading this book. Speak to them, and give them a desire to fully know your thoughts, your plans, and your ideas about every situation they encounter. Give them the ability to see with your eyes. Give them your thoughts and your understanding. Thank you, Lord, for being faithful to do this for them today. In Jesus' name, amen.

Verse to Remember: *For I will give you words and wisdom that none of your adversaries will be able to resist or contradict* (Luke 21:15).

Quote to Consider: Nine-tenths of wisdom is being wise in time. –Theodore Roosevelt[2]

Now, I implore you as a soldier of Jesus Christ, fight *the good fight...finish the race...*keep *the faith* (2 Timothy 4:7).

Three Hundred and Sixty Minutes

Theme: God's Inevitable Love

He has taken me to the banquet hall, and his banner over me is love.
Song of Solomon 2:4

The ancient folktale, *Rapunzel*, first written in the 3rd century and made popular in the early 1800's,[1] is a favorite tale of mine. While the story is quite long, the ending of the tale is what I find captivating. Rapunzel was claimed at birth by a cruel enchantress, who cast the beautiful Rapunzel into a high tower, locking her away so she would see no one. In order for the enchantress to get into the tower, she had to climb Rapunzel's long hair that hung out the window like a rope. Eventually, Rapunzel confessed that a young prince had also been climbing up to see her. When the enchantress heard of it, she cut Rapunzel's hair and forced her into a desert region. She then hung Rapunzel's hair from the tower so when the prince returned again, he would be tricked. And sure enough, when the prince climbed up to visit Rapunzel, the waiting witch threw him out. As he fell from the high tower, he landed in a thorn bush, which pierced his eyes and blinded him. In his sorrow and blindness he set out to wander in the desert. Years passed, and Rapunzel unexpectedly stumbled upon the love of her youth in the desert.

When she recognized it was her prince, she wept over him. As her tears dripped into his eyes, he was able to see again.[2]

Fairy tales appeal to us as children because we are enamored with the idea of someone being rescued by their lover. Humanity is an addict for proven affection. We desire love to be *displayed,* not just admitted. It derives from our innate need to be salvaged. But our human desires drive us to look for love in other places outside of God. There's something crucial we forget as humans—we forget that God is the only one who fervently longs for us, waits for us, and adores us. Instead of embracing the glory of God's care, we often pass off comments like, "Jesus loves you, God bless, and God is love."

Recognizing the love God has for you is part of being equipped for the spiritual battle. In order to have the radiance of God's love radiate from you, you must be filled with the knowledge of his great desire for you. You can't love like him, if you don't recognize his love for you. *"We love because he first loved us"* (1 John 4:19). When you let God weep over you, it will thrust you into advanced ministry.

In the same way Rapunzel met and wept over her lover, God meets you in your spiritual blindness and weeps over you. The love of the Lord gives you eyes to see, which is not only effective for ministry but also for decimating the darkness. Realization of God's adoration deflates the enemy's lies. Satan tries to make life look like a blurry, unfixable mess. He is quick to bury you in guilt, shame, and dread. He wants you to feel unappreciated, unnoticed, and uncared for. But that isn't the plan of God. God never meant for you to live an unfulfilled, sorrowful, and burdensome life. Understanding God's unlimited fondness for you is *imperative.* Lacking comprehension of the extent of God's love will keep you from total freedom, passionate ministry, and fanatic desire to spend time with him. You can't battle with wisdom, strength, and power if you are captive to doubting God's affection. Therefore I want to remind you of some aspects of God's adoration.

- God's love is unconditional; it's not based on your earthly success. While it's true that his blessings increase with your obedience, his affections for you are not a result of your actions. God has seen your failures, unfaithfulness, mean words, bitter heart, hidden affairs, perverted mind, scheming work, gossiping mouth, horrible attitude, your yearning to hate, your choice to slander, your refusal of truth, and your unjustified anger. Yet he love won't lessen; it *can't* lessen—

His love for you has always been full grown.

- God's love is unfailing. David says to the Lord, "*But I trust in your unfailing love; my heart rejoices in your salvation*" (Psalm 13:5). God's outrageous love isn't minuscule, momentary, or movable. God's adoration of humanity is not rooted in carnal principles. You can't flee the vastness of God's affection. His love will *always* come to save you. Every day God has lived he has loved you. His love stands strong when all else fades: "*At my first defense, no one came to my support, but everyone deserted me. May it not be held against them. But the Lord stood at my side and gave me strength...*" (2 Timothy 4:16-18).

- Lastly, his love is unflawed. In all ways, God's love for you is perfect. His delight for you is boundless and complete. Psalm 18:19 says, "*He brought me out into a spacious place; he rescued me because he delighted in me.*" Delight is the purest form of adoration. God's heart melts when he sees you! You are his little baby, crying about things you can't communicate, constantly being hungry for more, and making messes you can't clean up. But God delights in taking care of you. Only flawless love would make possible a flawless friendship. And he is a friend: "*Greater love has no one than this: to lay down his life for his friends*" (John 15:13).

It's hard to grasp the depth of his unconditional, unfailing, and unflawed love. However, if nothing in life can convince you of his desire for you, then you must remember the *unyielding* love he proved on the cross. Jesus hung on the cross for 6 hours, 360 minutes, and 21,600 seconds; which means that he had *21,600 seconds* to change his mind. But he chose you 21,600 times; now that's true bravery, compassion, and love! His desire for you is so passionate that his own skin could not contain all the love inside. No feeling of a whip, knife, or crown of thorns could combat the feeling of loss he would have had if he couldn't have claimed you. He put himself under you in order to catch your fall. And he fell onto a wooden cross. Even in his last breath he fought for your innocence by proclaiming: "*... 'Father, forgive them, for they do not know what they are doing'...*" (Luke 23:34). That's marvelous love, is it not?

Remember today that as you walk with the Lord he wants to fill you up with his overflowing, unconditional, unfailing, and flawless love. As you let him love on you, you will inevitably pour out that love upon the people around you. What a great God we serve! He is not only everything we need, but he is everything we can be!

Application:

Ask God today to reveal to you his love in a tangible way. Consider these questions about your allowance of God's affection in your life.

Can you remember a moment when you felt the most loved by God? What was happening? What did God do?

_____

_____

_____

_____

_____

_____

_____

What keeps you from focusing on the love of God? Do you feel like it's lies from the enemy or that you simply don't acknowledge all he does for you?

_____

_____

_____

_____

_____

_____

_____

_____

_____

_____

How often do you thank God for his love for you? How do you think thanking him more for his love in the small ways could help you see how much he loves you?

_____

_____

_____

_____

_____

Think of three ways God has loved you in the past couple of days even if they don't seem to be huge ways. Seriously take a look at your life. How has God made his love known to you?

-

-

-

You might say, "Janell, I don't feel God's love at all. I'm in the midst of being evangelical, but I'm really struggling to feel God's affection." If that is the case for you, spend some time today thinking about the cross. One time I forced myself to start counting seconds. I wanted to see if I could count to 21,600, the number of seconds Jesus was on the cross. I only got to about 200 before my eyes began to fill with tears, and a large lump of emotion entered my throat. Maybe you need to start counting the number of seconds Jesus hung on the cross for you. It truly will awaken your heart!

Remember God wants you to focus on his affection for you. It is a free gift! What strides can you make to focus more on God's love toward you?

_____

_____

_____

_____

_____

It's okay to tell God that you want him to make his love more evident. What situation(s) are you going through where you want God to reveal more of his love for you?

_____

_____

_____

_____

_____

_____

Verse to Remember: *...And I pray that you, being rooted and established in love, may have power, together with all the Lord's holy people, to grasp how wide and long and high and deep is the love of Christ, and to know this love that surpasses knowledge—that you may be filled to the measure of all the fullness of God* (Ephesians 3:17-19).

Quote to Consider: God has the right to be trusted; to be believed that He means what He says; and that His love is dependable. –A.J. Gossip[3]

Now, I implore you as a soldier of Jesus Christ, fight *the good fight...finish the race...keep the faith* (2 Timothy 4:7)

Day 23

One Suave God

Theme: God's Faithfulness

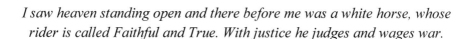

I saw heaven standing open and there before me was a white horse, whose rider is called Faithful and True. With justice he judges and wages war.

Revelations 19: 11

One extraordinary attribute of God is that he doesn't give up on people. It's easy to wonder if the good things we've done, the prayers we have prayed, the words we have said, the love we have showed, the brokenness we have felt will even make a difference at all. How can we just walk away from people and trust that it will all work out for them? How can we depart not knowing if they will be okay? How can we be certain and positive that everything is going to be fine in their lives? While it's good to be heartbroken and concerned for people, compassion can turn into unnecessary worry. The good news is that we don't have to be troubled! God consistently proves to be Jehovah-Shammah—the Lord who is present.[1] He has been present during each moment of your life. He's currently close, and he will be nearby in your future. He's the "*I AM*", the attentive lover, and the abiding friend (Exodus 3:14). It's tempting to believe that God might not be faithful simply because of how we feel, what we see, or what we *don't* see happening. However, God's faithfulness is seen all throughout scriptures; his enduring loyalty never ends (Psalm 119:90).

Throughout the Old Testament, there is an ongoing battle between God's people, the Israelites, and the tribe of Amalekite. The Amalekites were a wandering people. While their living regions were vast, the characteristics they portrayed were consistent: they were renowned for their cruel customs and mockery of the Israelite nation. Whenever an Amalekite was involved, there was some type of commotion taking place. The Amalekites always led a brutal charge against their enemies.[2]

God's frustration with the Amalekite tribe dated back to when they led an attack against the Israelites, who were coming out of Egypt. God's anger was not merely about the fact that the Amalekites attacked his people, but that they seized the people of God who were not strong enough to defend themselves. Another encounter that proves the brutality of the Amalekite tribe is found in 1 Samuel 30:11-13. This story involved an Amalekite and his Egyptian servant. The Amalekite master left his servant in a desert area for no reason other than being inconvenienced by his presence. Again, the obnoxious cruelty of the Amalekite tribe is revealed in 2 Samuel 1, when an Amalekite paraded through David's camp and gloated about how he had murdered Saul.

God's anger gave way to wrath, due to their evil ways. In Exodus 17:14, God says that he will "...*completely blot out the name of Amalek from under heaven.*" It was obvious that God had no tolerance for even Amalekite *possessions*. 1 Samuel 15:3 says that God desired "*all*" items of the Amalekites to be destroyed. One reason Saul lost his kingship was due to his disobedience in not slaughtering "*all*" of the Amalekites' goods. Saul let his men take the healthy sheep and cattle that belonged to the Amalekites. But that wasn't what God had commanded. Despite the advancement of the Amalekites, God was always present with his people, and he conquered his enemies with mighty blows.

Moving forward throughout scripture, you bump into the story of Esther, an Israelite girl who helped save her people by becoming queen and boldly pleading for mercy from King Xerxes. A commonly overlooked part in this story is the heroic actions of Esther's uncle, Mordecai. Mordecai determined his life to only be lived for the glory of God. When Haman, the antagonist, ordered that all men bow to him, Mordecai refused to be part of those who would bow. The interesting and important fact here is that Haman was an Agagite, which is another name for an Amalekite.[2] Mordecai knew about the cruel past and ways of the Amalekite nation. However, Mordecai trusted that God would save him, just as God had in the past. And God did prove true; the Israelite people were saved from Haman's evil plots to destroy them. In the end, *Haman* received the death penalty of being "*impaled... on the pole*", which he had purposed for the death of Mordecai and God's people (Esther 7:10).

The Scriptures prove God's majesty and faithfulness when it comes to his people. It's especially vital to note that, chronologically, Esther was the last book written in the Old Testament.[2] How suave of God to not only save his people all throughout their struggles, but to end their fight with great victory! Likewise, God will take care of the things you can't finish. He is there. He is present. He is moving, working, and loving on people when you can't due to your absence. God won't stop drawing in and ministering to the people you've poured into. Not only is this lesson of God's faithfulness vital for remembering God's unending work in others, but God is faithfully working in you as well.

You, like Mordecai, know your greatest enemy. According to scripture, Satan is constantly against you (1 Peter 5:8). But you don't have to bow your knee to his desires over your life. Satan, like the Amalekites, is the first to oppose you every day when you wake up. Revelations 12:10 says that Satan will accuse you all "*day and night*". Satan is against you, and he always will be. If you feel weary from battle, remember that God is on your battle field, and he is fighting for you. Deuteronomy 20:4 says, "*For the LORD your God is the one who goes with you to fight for you against your enemies to give you victory.*'" Then Jesus said in Matthew 11:28, "'*Come to me, all you who are weary and burdened, and I will give you rest.*" Resting in the arms of your Savior is the best place to be. You will be saved from the onslaught of the enemy because God wins. Period. It doesn't matter how many times your enemy, the devil, comes against you; the point, my friends, is that God *always* wins. He conquered the Amalekite tribe in the beginning, and he triumphed at the end of the Old Testament period as well. Similarly and symbolically, God used the cross to conquer your enemy before you were even born. Up until this very day, this very second, your enemy is still powerless against you. God has been faithful; he's been suave in the warfare.

"'*Listen to me, you descendants of Jacob, all the remnant of the people of Israel, you whom I have upheld since your birth, and have carried since you were born. Even to your old age and gray hairs I am he, I am he who will sustain you. I have made you and I will carry you; I will sustain you and I will rescue you*" (Isaiah 46:3-4).

Application:

Maybe you can look back over your life, and see where your enemy has been cruel, taunting, or vindictively vicious. How did God prove himself faithful during those times?

_____

_____

_____

_____

_____

_____

_____

_____

_____

_____

Are there battles you feel you are trying to fight on your own? What are they?

_____

_____

_____

_____

_____

_____

_____

_____

_____

_____

_____

_____

_____

_____

In what ways does reading about God's faithfulness in defeating the Amalekite tribe encourage you in your battles?

_____

_____

_____

_____

_____

_____

_____

_____

_____

_____

Have you found yourself bowing to the enemy's desires for your life? In what areas?

_____

_____

_____

_____

_____

_____

_____

_____

_____

_____

Do you find yourself worried about God's continued work in other people's lives? If so, look up Philippians 1:6; what does this verse tell you about God's character?

_____

_____

_____

_____

Let God have control of your situations, and let God help you win the battles you encounter.

Verse to Remember: *"But the Lord is faithful, and he will strengthen you and protect you from the evil one"* (2 Thessalonians 3:3).

Quote to Consider: A faithful friend is a strong defense; And he that hath found him hath found a treasure. – Louisa May Alcott[3]

Now, I implore you as a soldier of Jesus Christ, fight *the good fight...finish the race...*keep *the faith* (2 Timothy 4:7).

Day 24

Without Borders

Theme: Evangelizing Everywhere

Multitudes, multitudes in the valley of decision! For the day of the LORD is near in the valley of decision.

Joel 3:14

"On January 12, 1723, I made a solemn dedication of myself to God, and wrote it down; giving up myself, and all that I had to God; to be of the future, in no respect, my own; to act as one that had no right to be himself, in any respect. And solemnly vowed to take God for my whole portion and felicity; looking on nothing else, as any part of my happiness." – Jonathan Edwards.[1]

Jonathan Edwards played a monumental role in bringing forth the Great Awakening in Northampton, Massachusetts. He preached with fervor and zeal, and he was ultimately broken over mankind's spiritual condition. In 1733, Edwards was deeply concerned over the church of God, so he began preaching a new series of sermons. He hoped they would spark an awakening of the spiritually dead, and they did. His sermons led to the beginning of the Great Awakening in 1735, but it wasn't until 1740 that the full blast of the Great Awakening really struck the church. One hundred fifty churches were affected by the Awakening within a three-year time span.[2]

Edwards claimed missionary status right where he was. He unashamedly proclaimed the name of Jesus Christ. Edwards' teachings were powerful because they weren't mere talk; they were his life. He lived to please the Lord.[2] The concept of giving up personal rights in order to focus on God was also desired by John, Jesus' beloved disciple. *"He must become greater; I must become less "* (John 3:30). But what does that mean? What does it mean to make God *"become greater"*? It's about a personal resolve to take up God's cause and to lay down our own. It's about making his life and desires more important than our own.

Sometimes it's easy for a missionary to leave the international mission field, and wonder why God doesn't seem to move in their hometown. But God isn't the one not moving. You can rest assured that spiritually stagnant people aren't a result of God not calling or wanting them. God doesn't change his desire for mankind to know him. Jesus said, *"And I, when I am lifted up from the earth, will draw all people to myself "* (John 12:32).

Although God draws mankind, he graciously calls on you to be a part of his kingdom advancement. You are a vessel of God; you carry Christ within your flesh. When you leave one mission field, you simply enter another mission field; each place you step is another place to spread the gospel. You are a missionary without borders, a speaker of truth regardless of the region you are in. Simply because you shift lands doesn't mean that you shift revelations; the revelation is that Christ is in you, and you are to share him with the world. God's idea was that you, with him, would reach out to the *entire* world. Can you imagine what revival would take place if you asked God to break your heart for your family, friends, and coworkers like you asked him to break your heart for the nations? God's heart aches for people in your hometown. You don't have to be a missionary *overseas* to be labeled a missionary. You are a missionary no matter where you are. You carry the mission inside of your heart: the mission of loving lost souls to Jesus Christ.

Making goals about areas of your life you want to change upon returning home is normal and good. But it's easy to relapse into old, familiar cycles. Routines can be deadly because they are a suction cup of complacence. Temptation to remain inactive in proclaiming the gospel is partially caused by former habits. Human habits have never been easily altered. That's why it's so hard to jump-start new activities, diets, books, jobs… We are beings of habitual dealings. Wouldn't it be fanatical to capture the habit of talking to people about Jesus everywhere we went?!

You might not automatically feel compelled to witness to coworkers and neighbors. But being a witness is not an *option*; being a witness is the *calling*. It's tempting to feel more like a missionary overseas simply because it's a vastly different culture; you're witnessing yourself and others changing, and it's a wonderful, transforming experience! But there are advantages to reaching people in your hometown.

Part of the reason Christianity spread rapidly, during the times of the early church, was due to the common language shared all the way from India to Italy[3]. Matching language accessibility is a major advantage. You can communicate without a translator. What a blessing! It's also to your advantage that you see the same people daily. Forming deep and lasting relationships is a huge step to speaking into someone's life. Your family, friends, and coworkers will recognize you as the light; that will enable you to speak directly to their wounded areas and confusing circumstances.

It's important to question your heart as to the reason you may shy away from witnessing. It's vital to know your motives. Is it fear of rejection? Does it feel too difficult or overwhelming? Will it consume too much time? Or maybe you don't know how to start the conversation. A common reason for inactivity in witnessing can be due to having a nonconfrontational personality. We want to be politically correct. We don't want things to get messy, complex, or distorted, so we remain silent. However, God didn't come to make a pretty scene; Jesus was mauled, pierced, and flesh fell from his body "*...his appearance was so disfigured beyond that of any man and his form marred beyond human likeness—* " (Isaiah 52:14)! An innocent man was crucified; there is nothing politically correct about that. Check your heart and listen to God's leading. He will nudge your heart to speak. He knows the future and the responses people will have toward you. Witnessing is a part of trusting his timing and his call for you to speak. People want to be loved; their souls are the shape that fit God's name.

Remember that along with witnessing, prayer is vital. Here are some specific prayers to pray while in your hometown:

- First, ask God to shape your heart for the people who live around you. Ask him to provoke your heart to burn, yearn, and ache for the people.
- Ask God for divine appointments—heavenly opportune moments to share the gospel.

- Ask God for wisdom on the timing and words you use.
- Ask God to prepare your way by convicting your friends, families, and coworkers' hearts (Jude 1:15). Pray that through you they will feel God's love.

Application:

Who are some people you know who need the Lord? Maybe it's some of the same names you listed on the intercession day. Whoever they are, list them:

-
-
-
-
-
-
-
-

Okay now, go back. Next to each name on the list, jot down a few words about how you think they would respond to the gospel.

How do your ideas about their possible response affect your witnessing? Ask God to bring Scriptural truths to your mind in order to squash the fear that you have about sharing the good news with them.

_____

_____

_____

_____

_____

_____

_____

_____

_____

_____

_____

You can approach the topic of God with them without being intrusive. Maybe you need to communicate differently than you have in the past. How can you change the conversations from being superficial to spiritual?

_____

_____

_____

_____

_____

_____

_____

_____

_____

_____

_____

_____

_____

Go forth and conquer the souls that are right around you, and remember that you were purposed, called, for such a time as the one you are living. I charge you to not be afraid of possible rejection. People who discard you are actually pulling away from the love of God through you; it's not personal—it's _warfare_.

Verse to Remember: *"But whoever looks intently into the perfect law that gives freedom, and continues in it—not forgetting what they have heard, but doing it—they will be blessed in what they do"* (James 1:25).

Quote to Consider: The church that does not evangelize will fossilize. - Oswald J. Smith[4]

Now, I implore you as a soldier of Jesus Christ, fight *the good fight...finish the race...*keep *the faith* (2 Timothy 4:7).

Day 25

Unstoppable Romance

Theme: Continuation of a Seeking Heart

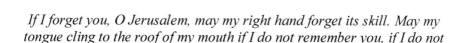

If I forget you, O Jerusalem, may my right hand forget its skill. May my tongue cling to the roof of my mouth if I do not remember you, if I do not consider Jerusalem my highest joy.

Psalm 137:5-6

Yesterday you read about the influence of Jonathan Edwards' role in revitalizing the church during the 1700's; the movement referred to as The Great Awakening took place in America and spread into Europe. A routine of Edwards' life, which I left out, was that Edwards spent over twelve hours a day reading scripture, writing, and studying godly wisdom and knowledge.[1] This fact is probably the most crucial aspect of Jonathan Edwards' life. Without his time with God, he would have not been able to reach the world. Being crazy in love with God is what makes the lost able to see his light in us.

Reaching the world is a division of the first and "*the most important*" call, which is to "*love the Lord*" (Mark 12:29-30). Remaining in the Lord is making sure that your relationship with God is not neglected and making sure your alone time with God is not preoccupied with everyday tasks. Jesus didn't ignore the importance of spending time with God. Luke 5:16 says, "*But Jesus often withdrew to lonely places and prayed.*" Jesus did not only *practice* spending time with God; he *taught* about remaining ready to see the

Father through this parable:

"At that time the kingdom of heaven will be like ten virgins who took their lamps and went out to meet the bridegroom. Five of them were foolish and five were wise. The foolish ones took their lamps but did not take any oil with them.The wise ones, however, took oil in jars along with their lamps. The bridegroom was a long time in coming, and they all became drowsy and fell asleep.

"At midnight the cry rang out: 'Here's the bridegroom! Come out to meet him!'

"Then all the virgins woke up and trimmed their lamps. The foolish ones said to the wise, 'Give us some of your oil; our lamps are going out.'

"'No,' they replied, 'there may not be enough for both us and you. Instead, go to those who sell oil and buy some for yourselves.'

"But while they were on their way to buy the oil, the bridegroom arrived. The virgins who were ready went in with him to the wedding banquet. And the door was shut.

"Later the others also came. 'Lord, Lord,' they said, 'open the door for us!'

"But he replied, 'Truly I tell you, I don't know you.'

"Therefore keep watch, because you do not know the day or the hour (Matthew 25:1-12).

It might be tempting to call those virgins crazy for falling asleep on the Lord. But, in truth, maybe you yourself get side tracked with life and forget to keep your candle burning. I know I've done it! I am guilty of having slacked off in my relationship with God, and eventually I became so spiritually unconscious that I couldn't even see how far away from him I had walked. The virgins in Matthew 25 had all the oil they needed. Your oil is the Word of God that fills the lamp, which is your heart. You've got to fuel the Word of God into your soul, or your fire will go out.

When I was a young girl, we would buy small bouncy ball toys. The enjoyment of the toys was that they could glow in the dark. However, I had to stand there and hold the ball up to a light for a long time before it would actually glow; that aspect was not necessarily fun. But once I shut off the lights, the end result was worth it all! Unfortunately, the light would eventually go out. You and I are like those glow-in-the-dark toys. We can't shine in the dark if we don't draw the source of our light from a higher power. God aches for us to spend time with him; he wants to light us up! You are the blaze of the Lord, but a fire can't remain lit without care. It's more than just about being a light to other people; it's about staying close to that love relationship with God.

In Revelations 2:3-4, God reveals his disapproval of mankind's forgetfulness to spend time with him by rebuking the Church of Ephesus: *"You have persevered and have endured hardships for my name, and have not grown weary. Yet I hold this against you: You have forsaken the love you had at first. Consider how far you have fallen! Repent and do the things you did at first. If you do not repent, I will come to you and remove your lampstand from its place."* He began his letter to the Church of Ephesus with the success they had achieved. Unfortunately, their downfall was forgetting the love they first had for the Lord. God confronted the Church of Ephesus when they had *"forsaken the love"* they *"had at first"*, and God told them to *"do the things"* they *"did at first."* Therefore, it's obvious that the *"things"* they *"did at first"* were actions that pulled them closer to God. He is heartbroken over his people, and he is a *"jealous God"* (Joshua 24:19). God notices when his people don't remain close to him. Unrequited love is agonizing. Your first created purpose was to belong to God. *"Jesus replied: '"Love the Lord your God with all your heart and with all your soul and with all your mind." This is the first and greatest commandment"* (Matthew 22:37-38).

Through the blood of Christ, romance with the Lord is destined for success. You will make evident the relationships you consider important. Jesus said, *"For where your treasure is, there your heart will be also"* (Luke 12:34). Failure to seek God will generate a loss of spiritual zeal. Remember that the maintenance of mere acquaintance with the Lord won't fulfill your soul; Jesus prayed, *"Give us today our daily bread"* (Matthew 6:11). And Solomon said, *"Keep falsehood and lies far from me; give me neither poverty nor riches, but give me only my daily bread"* (Proverbs 30:8). Although Solomon was talking about authentic bread, you can view this verse as being spiritual *"daily bread"*. According to scripture, Jesus is the *"bread of life"* (John 6:35); therefore, you need God-your-bread every day.

Steps to assist the art of remaining:

- Find a place for just you and God. Ask God to show you a "him and you" spot. Keeping a regular place helps you stay focused. Your "God place" may be in a park, your bedroom, or even your car.
- Figure out what time of day is best for you and the Lord. Make a point to seek him at a time when you are most attentive. A mentor of mine said that I should give God the best time of my day. What time of day do you think would be best for you and God?
- Next, ask God to make you hungry for spiritual growth. When you are physically hungry, you get something to eat. Ask him to make you spiritually famished so you will eat your "*daily bread.*"

Check your life. What strides are you making to advance spiritually? List them:

-

-

-

-

How does it make you feel to know that God longs for you to spend time with him?

_____

_____

_____

_____

_____

_____

_____

_____

_____

_____

God's letter to the Church of Ephesus said they had *"forsaken the love"* they *"had at first."* And he told them to *"do the things"* they *"did at first."* Maybe you used to have a habit of spending time with God and fell away from it. What actions can you take to make God your number one treasure?

_____

_____

_____

_____

_____

_____

Remember, the Lord promised if you would call on him he would answer you, and he would be there for you.

Verse to Remember: *"But if from there you seek the LORD your God, you will find him if you seek him with all your heart and with all your soul"* (Deuteronomy 4:29).

Quote to Consider: We have lost the sacred art of spending time with God, and nothing else can ever take its place. No repentance however deep, no restitution however costly, no sorrow however complete, can do away with the necessity for a daily time of sacred quiet, alone with God." (Keswick 1946)– Gordon M. Guinness[2]

Now, I implore you as a soldier of Jesus Christ, fight *the good fight...finish the race...*keep *the faith* (2 Timothy 4:7).

Day 26

Divine Persistence

Theme: Maintaining Relentless Prayer

The widow who is really in need and left all alone puts her hope in God and continues night and day to pray and to ask God for help. But the widow who lives for pleasure is dead even while she lives.

1 Timothy 5:5-6

Besides remaining devoted to witnessing and spending time with God, being unwavering and zealous in your prayer life is a colossal aspect of your Christian walk. Persistent prayer portrays the amount of desperation you have about a subject. Asking God something more than once does not mean that you doubt his ability to move. It does not mean that you believe he didn't hear you the first time, and it does not mean you think he lacks the desire to act. Persistent prayer is about keeping something before the Lord; it's an act of confidence in God's ability to work in every situation.

God's faithfulness to hear you and have compassion for you are claimed in the Scriptures: *"Because of the LORD's great love we are not consumed, for his compassions never fail. They are new every morning; great is your faithfulness. I say to myself, 'The LORD is my portion; therefore I will wait for him'"* (Lamentations 3:22-24). Recognizing God's faithfulness to answer your prayers and choosing to continuously pray are defined as active waiting. When you wait in line or at the doctor's office, you choose if you want to be inactive or not. But simply because you are expected to wait does not mean that you are expected not to move— hence, the magazines, books, and toys in the doctor's office and packages, goodies, and knickknacks to look at in a check-out line. Likewise, while you are waiting on God to answer, you don't have to be inactive in your prayers. It was a command that you should *"pray continually,"* (1 Thessalonians 5:17). God never wants, expects, or asks you to stop talking to him! God desires you to have an outrageously *obsessive* prayer life. He never wants what you think, do, or see to deter you from praying.

God's ways are not your ways (Isaiah 55:9); he is totally original in his answers to your prayers. He doesn't always answer in a way you might recognize. Because God and humanity don't always share the same ideas about good outcomes, God's answers are often mistaken for a lack of his caring. It's easy to not recognize gifts from God, just like when the world didn't recognize Jesus. They thought Jesus wasn't a good enough gift; they believed he'd come in shining robes and would have a staff of gold in his hands. Jesus was the most unconventional gift and yet the greatest gift mankind could ever ask for.

In what ways have you seen God fulfill your prayers in unexpected ways? Can you think of a specific time?

_____

_____

_____

_____

_____

_____

_____

_____

_____

_____

_____

_____

_____

"If you, then, though you are evil, know how to give good gifts to your children, how much more will your Father in heaven give good gifts to those who ask him!" (Matthew 7:11). Persistent prayer reveals faith that God can and wants to perform powerfully on behalf of his children. God wants to give good gifts to you! Little children persist in asking their parents for candy because they believe their parents can and want to give them good gifts; they are hoping that they will strike a cord of compassion and will get the yummy sweet. Kids know that their parents plan and desire to take care of them. When you ask God for something, according to his Word, you can know that God's plan is to answer your request.

Elijah, an Old Testament prophet, understood that God could not only save mankind from spiritual death, but that God *wanted* to be their physical healer. Elijah also realized that there was power in persistent prayer. In 1 Kings 17, Elijah was heartbroken that a widow's son had died, and Elijah responded to the situation with unrelenting prayer: *"'Give me your son,' Elijah replied. He took him from her arms, carried him to the upper room where he was staying, and laid him on his bed. Then he cried out to the LORD, 'O LORD my God, have you brought tragedy also upon this widow I am staying with, by causing her son to die?' Then he stretched himself out on the boy three times and cried to the LORD, 'O LORD my God, let this boy's life return to him!' The LORD heard Elijah's cry, and the boy's life returned to him, and he lived. Elijah picked up the child and carried him down from the room into the house. He gave him to his mother and said, 'Look, your son is alive!"* (V. 19-23).

Elijah cried out and laid his body on the boy *"three times"*. How vulnerable, how splendidly fanatical of him to stretch himself out over the boy not knowing if the boy would live. Maybe the people downstairs were mocking him, maybe they were even getting angry with him because they thought that he was being facetious, slanderous, and uncouth. Or maybe they were hopeful and shocked, because they'd never heard anyone cry out to God so persistently and with such fervor before. Elijah didn't know how the people would respond, but he did what was right—he prayed.

Prayer is a battle. Colossians 4:12 says, *"Epaphras, who is one of you and a servant of Christ Jesus, sends greetings. He is always wrestling in prayer for you, that you may stand firm in all the will of God, mature and fully assured."* How beautiful it is to wrestle with God! Jacob unashamedly wrestled all night with God; he wouldn't let God leave unless God blessed him. *"Then the man said, 'Let me go, for it is daybreak.' But Jacob replied,*

'I will not let you go unless you bless me'" (Genesis 32: 26). Doesn't it seem odd that God would want you to wrestle him? But it's quite the contrary; God trains you to be a warrior. He expects you to fight, and he anticipates you will battle using the tools he's given you. He's given you the tool of prayer.

Sometimes discouragement quickly approaches, when we can't see what we want. But maintaining a right attitude needs to accompany prayer warriors. *"You want something but don't get it. You kill and covet, but you cannot have what you want. You quarrel and fight. You do not have, because you do not ask God. When you ask, you do not receive, because you ask with wrong motives, that you may spend what you get on your pleasures"* (James 4:2-3). It's vital to put the essentials first in prayer: *"But seek first his kingdom and his righteousness, and all these things will be given to you as well"* (Matthew 6:33).

Remember that Satan works hard every day to keep the souls of the lost, but you can beat him at his own devices—pray tremendously outrageous prayers! You have the keys of the kingdom of heaven: God said, in Matthew 16:19, *"I will give you the keys of the kingdom of heaven..."* Don't fiddle with the keys; use them. Speak out what you desire; let Satan know what you're praying. He's so powerless to stop God from moving in your life.

"...The prayer of a righteous man is powerful and effective. Elijah was a man just like us. He prayed earnestly that it would not rain, and it did not rain on the land for three and a half years. Again he prayed, and the heavens gave rain, and the earth produced its crops" (James 5:16-18).

Application:

What is the most radical prayer request(s) you have?

_____

_____

_____

_____

_____

_____

_____

_____

_____

_____

_____

_____

_____

_____

_____

_____

_____

If God has not answered your request (s) yet, then remember to do some wrestling with him in prayer. How does knowing that God wants you to be a radical prayer warrior shape the way you pray?

_____

_____

_____

_____

_____

_____

_____

Look back to your prayer log on the day of intercession. Continue to pray for the people who you have met.

Remember that God also has dreams, goals, and wants—hone in on what God desires, and remember to be in prayer for those things as well! As God answers your prayers, come back to this page and write down, beside the prayers, the way God moved. Watch for God's unique answers. He is a creative God! Don't desist in your prayers; persist in your prayers!

Verse to Remember: *Be joyful in hope, patient in affliction, faithful in prayer* (Romans 12:12).

Quote to Consider: The one concern of the devil is to keep Christians from praying. He fears nothing from prayerless studies, prayerless work and prayerless religion. He laughs at our toil, mocks at our wisdom, but trembles when we pray. – Samuel Chadwick[1]

Now, I implore you as a soldier of Jesus Christ, fight *the good fight...finish the race...*keep *the faith* (2 Timothy 4:7).

Day 27

The Fruit Bearer

Theme: Living a Tasteful Life

This is to my Father's glory, that you bear much fruit, showing yourselves to be my disciples.

John 15:8

I watched her. She went for it. The strawberry looked fresh, juicy, and sweet. But her pure delight ended unexpectedly by the appearance of a small gray worm, popping its head out to claim its half-eaten territory.

Fruit is delicious; it's sweet, nutritious, and a burst of goodness. Unfortunately, for my friend, the fruit she chose to almost eat was not as insect-free as she desired. Fruit was created to be appetizing because it's good for us. However, when fruit is spoiled, ugly, and old, it's unappealing. There is a type of fruit that God and others have to taste; it's the fruit we cultivate in our hearts.

Jesus said that people will know who we are by the fruitfulness of our lives: "*Thus, by their fruit you will recognize them*" (Matthew 7:20). That is a huge responsibly. However, part of maintaining the call to reach the world for Christ is reaching inside of ourselves and digging out anything that would be a road block to other people's view of Christ. This is more than simply dealing with hidden, unconfessed sin. This is dealing with the attitude of the heart, the growth of our spiritual lives.

I wonder what type of taste God gets when he samples the fruit off the trees in my heart. I wonder if they are almost ripe, ready for harvest, or rotting. Do you wonder that about yourself? As Christians, we should be the first to check our hearts, but it's easy to get lazy when it comes to testing our fruit condition. It's so much easier to give in to our bad moods, lame excuses, and selfish emotions. I, pathetically, tend to use the excuse that I'm "not a morning person" in order to escape the excellence that comes with bearing fruit. I'm renowned for proclaiming that, until 10 a.m., I'm not "saved" yet. Mornings are the period of my day when it takes the most labor to keep my fruit ripe and sweet. My family will concur.

It's important to remember that other people have to sample the fruit that we cultivate in our hearts. Jesus said that all people would be able to tell a person's character by the spiritual fruit they exude… And he gave specific instructions for how to maintain the fruit of the Spirit in your inner being. What does John 15:4-5 say about how to maintain the fruit of holiness?

_____

_____

Good character doesn't go unnoticed. The early Christians were renowned for not only preaching with their personal experiences; they were also so kind to the unbeliever that it caused those who were outside of God to question their own faith. During the time of the early church, an epidemic burst forth in Alexandria leaving many for dead. While almost all people deserted those who were dying, the Christians came to nurture and to give proper burials for those who had passed.[1]

Bearing good fruit isn't a concept that ended during the early church days. In the 8th century, there lived a man named Charles, nicknamed Charles Martel (also known as Charles the Hammer). He was the son of Pippin II, who governed for 27 years over Frankish kingdoms. Charles is known for his victory in Spain in 732 A.D. This defeat was momentous because it halted the Islam faith from entering territory in Europe and France. By his successful conquest, he was regarded as the champion of Christian Europe.[2] Not only did he achieve great defeats, but he made another interesting move—he sent missionaries all throughout vast Europe! The key factor in this excursion is not where he sent the missionaries but *why* he sent them. Charles was so impressed with the way the Christians behaved in his kingdom that he wanted all citizens to have attitudes like the Christians!

Charles saw a difference between the unbeliever and the believer.[3] It's easy to forget that people can see a difference between our lives and the lives of those who don't know God.

Isn't making an impact for Christ one of the goals of our faith? How amazing for the Christians in Charles's empire to live such wonderful lives in the eyes of their king that they inspired him to spread the gospel. That is fanatic resolve living, for sure! The fact that those Christians made it easy for Charles to govern them says something about the way they lived their lives. That's an awesome reputation to achieve—being the easiest to rule *because* you are a peacemaker. If the 8th century Christians would have not responded to the call to bear fruit, ultimately they would have never been able to reach all of Europe. By their choosing to bear good fruit, they ended up being able to touch their world.

Paul wrote in Colossians that by the wisdom and knowledge of the Lord, one is filled with the strength to bear fruit: *"For this reason, since the day we heard about you, we have not stopped praying for you. We continually ask God to fill you with the knowledge of his will through all the wisdom and understanding that the Spirit gives, so that you may live a life worthy of the Lord and please him in every way: bearing fruit in every good work, growing in the knowledge of God, being strengthened with all power according to his glorious might so that you may have great endurance and patience"* (Colossians 1:9-11).

Just as the worm was revealed to my friend, the true condition of your fruit will be revealed. Remaining in God is the path to cultivating good fruit in your life. If fruit trees are blighted, insect infested, and decomposing, that is a sign of them needing more sunlight, water, and pruning. Likewise, if you see that your fruit is unappealing and stagnant in growth, you probably need more of the Son's light, his waters of healing, and his pruning or correction to help mature your lifestyle.

Ask God to reveal which fruit of the Spirit he wants you to work on this moment, day, and week. Remember that every day the people around you have to sample the fruit of your heart. I hope they find it to be ripe, fresh, and sweet.

Application:

Here is a Fruit Exam: sample your fruit, and circle which number you think best represents your fruit condition. On a scale from 1-10 (1 being low, 10 being high), circle your fruit-growth progress. Think about specific times when you've needed that fruit. What did you do? Pray about it; ask God to show you your heart, and ask him to "*search*" you (Psalm 139:23).

"*But the fruit of the Spirit is love, joy, peace, forbearance, kindness, goodness, faithfulness, gentleness and self-control. Against such things there is no law*" (Galatians 5:22-23).

Love. When you are presented with a difficult person or circumstance, how great is your love toward them?

1   2   3   4   5   6   7   8   9   10

Joy. In the midst of troublesome times, or even on a day-to-day basis, what does your joy meter look like?

1   2   3   4   5   6   7   8   9   10

Peace. Are you at rest with the things God is doing in your life? How much peace do you exude?

1   2   3   4   5   6   7   8   9   10

Forbearance (patience). Things don't always go our way; how long-lasting is your patience? Do you show it often?

1   2   3   4   5   6   7   8   9   10

Kindness. What are your thoughts like? What is your attitude toward others? Are you as kind as you could be?

1   2   3   4   5   6   7   8   9   10

Goodness. Do you exhibit the sweet presence of God in your life? Would someone look at you and say that you are a pleasure to be around?

1   2   3   4   5   6   7   8   9   10

Faithfulness. How faithful are you with the things God has given you to do?

1   2   3   4   5   6   7   8   9   10

Gentleness. It's hard to be gentle with other people when we let pride in. Are you gentle with other people's feelings despite their character flaws?

1   2   3   4   5   6   7   8   9   10

Self-control. Are you willing to die to self on a daily basis?

1   2   3   4   5   6   7   8   9   10

Do you see what needs pruning in your life? Ask God to faithfully remind you of that fruit and to give you situations where you can work that fruit into growth. I know that through Christ you can do it! I believe in your ability to hold yourself accountable to the things you've learned of Christ.

> # Verse to Remember: *The righteous will flourish like a palm tree, they will grow like a cedar of Lebanon ;planted in the house of the LORD, they will flourish in the courts of our God. They will still bear fruit in old age, they will stay fresh and green,* (Psalm 92:12-14).
>
> # Quote to Consider: The purpose of life is not to be happy - but to *matter*, to be productive, to be useful, to have it make some difference that you have lived at all. – Leo Rosten[4]

Now, I implore you as a soldier of Jesus Christ, fight *the good fight...finish the race...*keep *the faith* (2 Timothy 4:7).

Day 28

An "*Even If*" Attitude

Theme: Being Content with God's decisions

For I hear many whispering, "Terror on every side!" They conspire against me and plot to take my life. But I trust in you, LORD; I say, "You are my God."

Psalm 31:13-14

It's obvious when someone is lagging in being prepared for the day. When an individual claims to be ready to leave the house, but doesn't have their shoes on, you know that you'll be in for a bit longer wait. Shoes are normally one of the final details to getting ready. Likewise, when someone is spiritually ready for battle, you will know they are fully prepared once they have their warrior shoes intact. The Bible refers to these spiritual battle shoes as the "...*feet fitted with... readiness*" (Ephesians 6:15).

Having prepared feet is vital to answering the call of God. Not only do the feet of readiness ensure that you're prepared to battle spiritually, but it speaks about your heart condition— it says that you're at peace. Ephesians 6:15 says that, "...*feet fitted with the readiness... comes from the gospel of peace.*"

Peace is birthed from the understanding of what God's character is like no matter the situation you're dealing with. Peace derives from total trust of God's abilities to do the right thing on your behalf. When you comprehend who God is, you see that his ways are better, higher, and more advanced compared to your finite, blurry definition of the word "good" (Isaiah 55:9). Godly peace isn't based on *circumstance*; it's based on *trust*. It's rooted in belief of God's love over your life. It's the surreal surrender.

When evangelizing, it's vital to have a daily encounter with this surrender that leads to peace. The hours must be a proclamation of, "I give up my wants." The minutes must consist of the continual cry, "My life all for my King!" And in between the sacrificial seconds, one's heart should proclaim, "*He must become greater; I must become less*" (John 3:30). But life is hard; it's complex, ridiculous, and irritating sometimes. Maintaining a peaceful heart does not mean that you will consistently thrive in restful situations. Shadrach, Meshach, and Abednego were faced with an extremely difficult situation in Daniel 3. They were told that they would either bow to the golden image King Nebuchadnezzar built, or they would be thrown into fire. If you know the story, then you know that they chose the flaming furnace over bowing to the idol that sat before them. Here is the amazing response they gave to the king when questioned about their refusal to bow down: ... "*O Nebuchadnezzar, we do not need to defend ourselves before you in this matter. If we are thrown into the blazing furnace, the God we serve is able to save us from it, and he will rescue us from your hand, O king. But even if he does not, we want you to know, O king, that we will not serve your gods or worship the image of gold you have set up*"(V. 16-18).

They said, "*...even if he does not...*" How powerful! They were willing to stand and obey God because they had full confidence that God would have his way, and that God was good. They were content in surrendering their lives to the God who loves them passionately. They knew God's character, and therefore they had peace in the midst of a situation where they might possibly die. Wouldn't it be amazing to live "*even if he does not*" lives?! There's no doubt that you will see both good and bad times. But you can preserve peace knowing that God is unceasingly good.

Dietrich Bonhoeffer, a German pastor, encountered death at the gallows on April 9, 1945. He radically served the Lord throughout his life. Even in the moments of his death he was subservient to God's call. His execution was witnessed by a doctor at the camp, who declared: "I saw Pastor Bonhoeffer ... kneeling on the floor praying fervently to God. I was most deeply moved by the way this lovable man prayed, so devout and so certain that God heard his prayer. At the place of execution, he again said a short prayer and then climbed the few steps to the gallows, brave and composed. His death ensued after a few seconds. In the almost fifty years that I worked as a doctor, I have hardly ever seen a man die so entirely submissive to the will of God."[1]

Bonhoeffer was not spared. But he didn't live to be *spared*; he lived to be a *servant* of God. It's hard to give ourselves over to unknown outcomes. However, Jesus hasn't called us to do something that he wasn't willing to do himself. The *"even if"* attitude is found in the life of Christ. God didn't save Jesus from pain. In Luke 22:42 Jesus says, *"'Father, if you are willing, take this cup from me; yet not my will, but yours be done'"* Jesus entrusted himself to God. If Jesus hadn't committed to possess ready feet, it would have been easy for him to become complacent and walk away from his ministry. But Jesus resolved to have ready feet, and his resolving gave way to submission.

I encourage you today to make a life-changing, feet-stabilizing commitment. Keep your peace (which is ignited through trust) that God is righteous, loving, and good. Remember that by embracing the *"even if he does not"* attitude, you are embracing godly submission. As a warrior of God, you need to uphold an attitude of readiness even when things aren't going the best. Being fitted with the feet of readiness is more than just about being okay with life; it's about the acceptance that God may lead you onto a path that isn't ideal. Are you ready to have an *"even if"* attitude?

Here are some common circumstances that call for surrendering:

- Even if he doesn't save my parent.
- Even if he doesn't spare my child.
- Even if he doesn't send me to the place I wanted to go.
- Even if he doesn't deliver the job I wanted.
- Even if he doesn't answer my prayer immediately.
- Even if he doesn't eliminate my marital troubles.
- Even if he doesn't keep me from getting ill.
- Even if he doesn't heal my friend.
- Even if he doesn't rescue me from persecution.
- Even if he doesn't bring back my spouse.
- Even if he doesn't have a mate for me.
- Even if he doesn't fix my financial situations.
- Even if he doesn't answer the way I wanted.

Application:

Now it's your turn. This is between you and God. Ask God what commitment you need to make to him today. What's your pledge to God?

Even if he does not…

Even if he does not…

Even if he does not…

Even if he does not…

Even if he does not…

Verse to Remember: *I eagerly expect and hope that I will in no way be ashamed, but will have sufficient courage so that now as always Christ will be exalted in my body, whether by life or by death. For to me, to live is Christ and to die is gain* (Philippians 1:20-21).

Quote to Consider: Never be afraid to trust an unknown future to a known God. – Corrie Ten Boom[2]

Now, I implore you as a soldier of Jesus Christ, fight *the good fight…finish the race…keep the faith* (2 Timothy 4:7).

Day 29

Approved at the Gate

Theme: Living like a Citizen of Heaven

Since you call on a Father who judges each person's work impartially, live out your time as foreigners here in reverent fear.

1 Peter 1:17

She said she was lonely. I looked over at her as she steadied her solemn eyes on the unlit country road. "Janell, I figured out why I'm so sad," she expressed with a deep pain that made me attentive to her every word. "I am sad because I want to go home."

"You want to move back to where you grew up?" I said.

"No," she replied, "I want my homeland. I think I'm lonely for heaven. Do you ever ache like that? For the place where your heart belongs?"

It's true that the land we walk on was never meant to be the home we stay in. We were destined for a much greater kingdom—the nation of heaven. We get so fixated on where we are that we forget we aren't *of* this place. Earth is not our address. In the same way that it's tempting to fall out of practice of actively sharing your faith and spending time with God, it's also tempting to merge back into carnal ways of living.

Even though your physical body wakes up in the world, the essence of who you are is not in the world. Abraham knew that God was preparing a better home for him that wasn't on this planet. *By faith he made his home in*

---

the promised land like a stranger in a foreign country; he lived in tents, as did Isaac and Jacob, who were heirs with him of the same promise. For he was looking forward to the city with foundations, whose architect and builder is God (Hebrews 11:9-10).

Just as you use a passport when entering into another national territory, you also were given a spiritual passport when you became a citizen of God's kingdom. *Consequently, you are no longer foreigners and strangers, but fellow citizens with God's people and also members of his household,* (Ephesians 2:19). Every day your passport is stamped with the world.

It's important to note that while you can obtain dual citizenship in the world, God doesn't believe in *spiritual* dual citizenship. You cannot be both of light and of the dark. You cannot straddle the fence, having one foot on the path that leads to life and the other foot on the worldly path that leads to death. Philippians 3:20 says "… *our citizenship is in heaven." W*hen you received your spiritual heavenly nationality, you were required to trade in your earthly passport.

You know when you hear music from another country. It has unusual beats, unique singers, and foreign instruments. You can also identify when someone is from a native place by their style. You can even hear someone's homeland through their accent. Likewise, if you're living in the time zone of heaven, then earthly living should appear unusual. Culture shock 101 will tell you that when you are in a new place you will feel out of your element. Living on earth will and ought to make a Christian feel out of place. You should sense the feeling of being incompatible with worldly living.

People don't change their cultural tendencies just because they cross into another country. They may learn new things from a different culture, but their concepts and values tend cling to them. In the same way, as we grow in the knowledge and love of God, we should let heaven's culture cling to us. We may have to give up carnal activities so that we look more like a national of heaven. The way we live on earth will say something about our attachment to our heavenly citizenship.

Citizenship is not just rights, but it's obligations. Active citizenship means living out the kingdom of God. It's important to make sure that the way you live your life reflects kingdom living. *"For you were once darkness, but now you are light in the Lord. Live as children of light"* (Ephesians 5:8). The definition of the word citizen is "a native or naturalized member of state or nation who owes allegiance to it's government and is entitled to its protection."[1] Every day you demonstrate allegiance to something. You bow or curtsey to the things you cherish. When you value heaven's customs, the King says he will bless and protect you (John 17:11).

The first form of citizenship was seen in ancient Greek culture. The term for their city was "polis." Ordinary life was highly connected to the responsibility of being a part of the polis. Citizenship was an obligation filled not only in the eye of the public but was even more about the concealed life of each person.[2] Jesus referenced this idea by holding mankind accountable for what they ponder in their hearts and minds (Mark 7:20).

Living the kingdom life is not only for the advancement of your relationship with God. You also want people to see God in you, as well. How will anyone know that you're a citizen of heaven if you act like you're a citizen of the world? If you can't check your actions in through the gate of heaven, then they probably aren't kingdom- approved. James 1:27 says, *"Religion that God our Father accepts as pure and faultless is this: to look after orphans and widows in their distress and to keep oneself from being polluted by the world."*

Charging ourselves to remain uncontaminated *"by the world"* is a huge task. It's not only about having a right heart before God, but it's about checking the items that entertain us within our homes. Test your belongings. Go through your closet, drawers, books, movies, and music; ask God if there is anything that does not reflect your soul's nationality. Wouldn't it be wonderful to have your home be an atmosphere of heaven?!

Application:

Seriously question yourself about your favorite genre of entertainment. Are there certain music, films, or books you enjoy that you know are not pleasing to the Lord? If you're not sure, check with God's Word to see what he teaches. Remember that any activity or entertainment which is not of God should feel foreign to your soul. Ask God to make you aware of the things that are not of his kingdom.

How can you make your home a place that looks more like heaven? What goals will you set for yourself?

_____

_____

_____

_____

_____

_____

_____

_____

_____

_____

_____

_____

Here are some ideas to reflect kingdom living in your home and life: hang or paint verses on the walls, tape verses to your mirror, or put them near your kitchen sink. If you struggle with a particular worldly song or TV show, put a Bible verse around your radio or TV. If you need to, put a little sticky note on the back of your iPod with a verse on it.

It also may be helpful to leave Christian music playing in order to dispel the darkness. Maybe retrieve some spiritual decorations so that as you walk through your house you are constantly reminded of your place in the world and who God is to you.

The irony about life is that the city which you let live in you will ultimately be the city you live in one day. If you let evil abide in you, then you will eternally abide in Satan's domain. If you let righteousness flourish in you, then you will eternally live with the King of Glory.

I encourage you to make sure that you are letting the kingdom of God shine in your life. Keep in mind that in most countries you cannot be a part of their military if you are currently serving in another country's forces.[3] So let your living reflect your desire to be in God's army. Ask God to help you reflect the lifestyle of heaven.

Verse to Remember: *But in keeping with his promise we are looking forward to a new heaven and a new earth, where righteousness dwells. So then, dear friends, since you are looking forward to this, make every effort to be found spotless, blameless and at peace with him* (2 Peter 3:13-14).

Quote to Consider: We are not only to renounce evil, but to manifest the truth. We tell people the world is vain; let our lives manifest that it is so. We tell them that our home is above and that all these things are transitory. Does our dwelling look like it? O to live consistent lives!— Hudson Taylor[4]

Now, I implore you as a soldier of Jesus Christ, fight *the good fight...finish the race...*keep *the faith* (2 Timothy 4:7).

The Radical Recollection

Theme: Remembering the Movements of God

Look to the LORD and his strength; seek his face always. Remember the wonders he has done, his miracles, and the judgments he pronounced,

1 Chronicles 16:11-12

It was around 33 A.D. Thirteen men sat around a table to have a dinner renowned as the Last Supper. This event signified the importance of remembering the sacrifice Jesus was about to perform on the cross. Jesus had them eat bread and drink wine to remember his body that would be broken and his blood that would be spilled. He said "*… do this in remembrance of me*'" (Luke 22:19). Eventually, this occasion became recognized as Communion. However, up until the third and fourth centuries A.D., the title for the Last Supper was actually "agape". This word derives from the Greek language and means love.[1] From this fact, we observe that the remembering (or cherishing the memory) of someone is often evidence of how much we love them. Likewise, loving God is rooted in remembering what he's done and who he has been.

There's something special about being kept in someone's loving thoughts. It's evidence of our role to them. We were made in the image of God, so it shouldn't surprise us that God also wants to be remembered. He feels special and loved when we remember what he's done for us. Many times in the scriptures, God said that he frequently remembered his people: "*…I have made you, you are my servant; Israel, I will not forget you*" (Isaiah 44:21). He wants us to consider him as well: "*Remember the former things, those of long ago; I am God, and there is no other; I am God, and there is none like me*" (Isaiah 46:9). Jesus knew that mankind was selfish in their thoughts; maybe that's why he made his final dinner about remembering. He already experienced his best friends forgetting miracles he had accomplished. He knew it was easy for mankind to disregard his actions. Jesus experienced it many times.

In Matthew 14, Jesus performed one of the most mysterious miracles of all time—he turned five loaves of bread and two fish into enough food to feed five thousand people! Not only did he provide enough for the crowd, but he provided *more* than they needed: *They all ate and were satisfied, and the disciples picked up twelve basketfuls of broken pieces that were left over* (Matthew 14:20). Could you imagine seeing something like that take place? Wouldn't that just astound you? The disciples suggested the people go buy food for themselves, but Jesus wanted to supply their needs.

It's inconceivable that one could forget a miracle like multiplied bread and fish. However, the disciples seemed to have had spiritual memory loss. Even after Jesus had fed the five thousand in Matthew 14, the disciples still lacked trust in Christ's ability to provide in Matthew 15. "*His disciples answered, 'Where could we get enough bread in this remote place to feed such a crowd?'*" (Matthew 15:33). How could the disciples so quickly forget that Jesus can do anything?! The crowd in Matthew 15 was not only smaller, but they also started off with more bread and fish than in Matthew 14! The disciples' forgetfulness had nothing to do with the size of the crowd; instead, they disregarded the size of God's ability, willingness, and faithfulness. They allowed their vision to control their faith. Jesus told them who he was. They had seen what he could do. But their fears distorted their remembrance.

God will hold us accountable for forgetting his power. It's ludicrous how quickly the disciples forgot what a mighty God they served. Unfortunately, the story of their forgetfulness doesn't end with their mishap in Matthew 15. In Matthew 16, they forgot again the miracles Jesus was able to perform. But this time, Jesus confronted the issue: "*Aware of their discussion, Jesus asked, 'You of little faith, why are you talking among yourselves about having no bread? Do you still not understand? Don't you remember the five loaves for the five thousand, and how many basketfuls you gathered? Or the seven loaves for the four thousand, and how many basketfuls you gathered?"* (Matthew 16:8-10). Jesus was nicer to them for doubting than I would have been. I probably would have yelled at them for being so scatterbrained, and then I would have not given them any bread at all! I'm kidding. But this is a peculiar moment in history that can serve to awaken us to our forgetfulness.

Satan doesn't want you to recall the ways God has moved in your life. Remembrance is a weapon that can put Satan in his place. When you force yourself to call into account the things that God has done in a situation, you crush the enemy's advances. Lies reveal the cowardliness of Satan. Satan can't even give specific reasons why you should be distressed. He just guides your mind into confusion in order to distract you from the ways God has moved. But cling to your testimony! Let your mind tightly clutch the ways God has been faithful! Your past can help you keep Satan under your feet. Your testimony overcomes the darkness. Your life lessons can be used to crush Satan's plans of darkness for your future.

God is the same yesterday, today, and forever. Your circumstances, geography, and desires may change, but God never changes. When you take into account the things he has done in your life, it can encourage you for the present and for the future. Asaph determines to remember the revolution of change in his life: *"I will remember the deeds of the LORD; yes, I will remember your miracles of long ago. I will meditate on all your works and consider all your mighty deeds. Your ways, O God, are holy. What god is so great as our God? You are the God who performs miracles; you display your power among the peoples"* (Psalm 77:11-14). Keep the things God has done close in your heart just as Mary hid the special things of life in her heart. *"But Mary treasured up all these things and pondered them in her heart"* (Luke 2:19).

Application:

Remembering what God has done in your life will hopefully spark a desire to share it with people. This can also be used as a witnessing mechanism. If you feel comfortable, I encourage you to tell someone the recent things God has done in your life. Maybe share them with your church, a best friend, or a family member. Just acknowledge to someone your certainty of God's fanatically faithful movements. *"We will not hide them from their children; we will tell the next generation the praiseworthy deeds of the LORD, his power, and the wonders he has done... so the next generation would know them, even the children yet to be born, and they in turn would tell their children. Then they would put their trust in God and would not forget his deeds but would keep his commands"* (Psalm 78: 4, 6-7).

There are several questions to go through below. Take your time to really think about the things God has done. This journaling section will help serve as a reminder of the ways you experienced God!

Take a moment and think back about the things God has done in the past or in the last 30 days. Is there something specific that happened which shifted your idea of who God is?

_____

_____

_____

_____

_____

_____

_____

_____

_____

_____

_____

_____

_____

_____

_____

_____

_____

_____

_____

_____

_____
_____
_____
_____
_____
_____
_____
_____
_____
_____

What is your favorite memory of your time with God in the last 30 days?

_____
_____
_____
_____
_____
_____
_____
_____
_____
_____
_____
_____
_____
_____
_____
_____

_____

_____

_____

If you could pick one attribute that God has faithfully used with you these past many weeks, what would it be? And why?

_____

_____

_____

_____

_____

_____

_____

_____

_____

Did you see God perform unexpected miracles? What were they?

_____

_____

_____

_____

_____

_____

_____

_____

_____

_____

_____

_____

_____

Who is the most memorable person you witnessed to in the course of your evangelism? What impact did they make on your life?

_____

_____

_____

_____

_____

_____

_____

_____

_____

What is the greatest lesson you learned about yourself?

_____

_____

_____

_____

_____

_____

_____

_____

_____

_____

What was your greatest struggle in sharing the gospel message? In what ways did that serve to shape your view of God and the life of Christ?

_____

_____

_____

_____

_____

_____

_____

_____

_____

Out of all things you read and all the scripture you studied, is there a verse that you would say defines your journey these last few weeks?

_____

_____

_____

_____

_____

_____

_____

_____

_____

_____

_____

_____

_____

_____

What commitments are you making to God about remaining close to him?

_____

_____

_____

_____

_____

_____

_____

_____

_____

Look back to the devotional on day 1. You wrote down one word that you wanted and needed God to be for you. How did you witness God fulfilling that one word statement?

_____

_____

_____

_____

_____

_____

_____

_____

_____

_____

_____

_____

If you could thank God for anything he has done for you in the past weeks, what would you want to thank him for?

_____

_____

_____

_____

_____

_____

_____

_____

_____

_____

_____

_____

_____

_____

_____

_____

_____

_____

_____

_____

_____

_____

_____

_____

_____

_____

_____

_____

Verse to Remember: *Remember the wonders he has done, his miracles, and the judgments he pronounced,* (Psalm 105:5).

Quote to Consider: Christ has no body on earth but yours, no hands but yours, no feet but yours. Yours are the eyes through which Christ's compassion for the world is to look out; yours are the feet with which He is to go about doing good; and yours are the hands with which He is to bless us now – Saint Teresa of Avila[2]

Now, I implore you as a soldier of Jesus Christ, fight *the good fight...finish the race*...keep *the faith* (2 Timothy 4:7). And finally I charge you to maintain a fanatic resolve to love, obey, and know God.

Journal

Reflections & Experiences

Prayer Log

Date :   Person Met:

Story about meeting:

_____

_____

_____

_____

_____

What to pray for them:

-

-

-

-

Date :   Person Met:

Story about meeting:

_____

_____

_____

_____

_____

What to pray for them:

-

-
-
-

Date :   Person Met:

Story about meeting:

_____

_____

_____

_____

_____

What to pray for them:

-
-
-
-

Date :   Person Met:

Story about meeting:

_____

_____

_____

_____

_____

What to pray for them:

-
-
-
-

Date :   Person Met:

Story about meeting:

_____

_____

_____

_____

_____

What to pray for them:

-
-
-
-

Date :   Person Met:

Story about meeting:

_____

_____

_____

_____

_____

What to pray for them:

-

-

-

-

Date :   Person Met:

Story about meeting:

_____

_____

_____

_____

_____

What to pray for them:

-

-

-

-

Date :   Person Met:

Story about meeting:

_____

_____

_____

_____

_____

_____

What to pray for them:

-
-
-
-

Date :   Person Met:

Story about meeting:

_____

_____

_____

_____

_____

What to pray for them:

-
-
-
-

Date :   Person Met:

Story about meeting:

_____

_____

_____

_____

_____

What to pray for them:

-

-

-

-

Date :   Person Met:

Story about meeting:

_____

_____

_____

_____

_____

What to pray for them:

-

-

-

-

Acknowledgements

Thank you to Diane Owen, Kathy Slone, and Nancy Ward for content revision, proofreading, and theological editing.

Many thanks to Dennis Linnell and Don Cady for support and direction during the writing process, and also to Lyn Rayn and Sam Justice for design.

And thanks to family and friends, especially Debra Crites, who supported me with prayers, listening ears, and encouragement.

You all have been an immense blessing.

Work Cited

Fellowship of Fire:

1. *Got Questions Ministries*. (2002-2011). Retrieved February 2, 2011, from http://www.gotquestions.org/apostles-die.html
2. *Think Exist*. (1999-2010). Retrieved February 15, 2011, from http://thinkexist.com/quotation/we-must-be-global-christians-with-a-global-vision/382570.html

Compassion Fashion:

1. Dowley, T., John, H., Robert, D., & David, F. (Eds). (2002). *Introduction to the history of Christianity* (pp. 430-431). Minneapolis: Augsburg Books.
2. Oceans of Grace. (2010). *Meditations & devotions on the ocean of God's sovereign grace*. Retrieved February 10, 2011, from http://oceanofgrace.org/2010/03/29/compassion-colored-everything-he-did/#axzz1Da1XMOiz

Your Personal Account:

1. Vos, H. F. (1999). *Nelson's new illustrated Bible manners & customs: How the people of the Bible really lived* (pp. 286, 383-385). Nashville: Thomas Nelson Inc.
2. *Famous quotes*. (n.d.). Retrieved February 9, 2011, from http://www.brainyquote.com/quotes/m/martinluth103526.html

Going Gallantly:

1. Britain Unlimited. (n.d.). *Grace Darling*. Retrieved January 12, 2011, from http://www.britainunlimited.com/Biogs/Darling.html

2. *Famous Quotes*. (n.d.). Retrieved January 11, 2011, from http://www.brainyquote.com/quotes/keywords/rememberin g.html

Ditching Death:

1. *Famous Quotes*. (n.d.). Retrieved January 28, 2011, from http://www.brainyquote.com/quotes/authors/a/abraham_lin coln.html
2. *Quote Garden*. (date).Retrieved February 9, 2011, from http://www.quotegarden.com/forgiveness.html

The Way We Tread:

1. *Ochristian.com.* (1999-2010). Retrieved February 9, 2011, from http://christian-quotes.ochristian.com/Meekness-Quotes/

The Commission to Cry:

1. *Ochristian.com.* (n.d.). Retrieved January 12, 2011, from http://christian-quotes.ochristian.com/Intercession-Quotes/

Growing Gold:

1. Vos, H.F. (1999). *Nelson's new illustrated Bible manners & customs: How the people of the Bible really lived* (p. 266). Nashville: Thomas Nelson Inc.
2. *Ehow.com.* (1999-2011). Retrieved January 2, 2011, from http://www.ehow.com/how-does_5001478_how-gold-refined.html
3. *Ochristian.com.* (1999-2010). Retrieved February 10, 2011, from http://christian-quotes.ochristian.com/Compassion-Quotes/page-3.shtml

Just Like Bullets:

1. Sherwood, C. (n.d.). *Your brain*. Retrieved February 2, 2011, from http://www.superteacherworksheets.com/human-body/brain.pdf
2. Vos, H.F. (1999). *Nelson's new illustrated Bible manners & customs: How the people of the Bible really lived* (p. 265). Nashville: Thomas Nelson Inc.
3. *Quote Garden*. (2010). Retrieved January 11, 2011, from http://www.quotegarden.com/thinking.html

Dissention in the Rank:

1. *Dictionary.com*. (2011). Retrieved February 2, 2011, from http://dicitonary.reference.com/browse/jostle
2. *Famous Quotes*. (n.d.). Retrieved January 2011, from http://www.brainyquote.com/quotes/authors/m/mother_teresa_2.html

Life Breather:

1. *Quote Garden*. (2010). Retrieved January 22, 2011, from http://www.quotegarden.com/helping.html

The Inevitable Persecution:

1. *Famous Quotes*. (n.d.). Retrieved January 21, 2011, from http://www.brainyquote.com/quotes/keywords/fruit_5.html

Worship Warrior:

1. *Famous Quotes*. (n.d.). Retrieved January 21, 2011, from http://www.brainyquote.com/quotes/keywords/praise_5.html

The Solo Soldier:

1. *Brighthub.* (2011). Retrieved February 2, 2011, from http://www.brighthub.com/education/early-childhood/articles/46842.aspx
2. *Wondertime.* (n.d.). Retrieved February 2, 2011, from http://wondertime.go.com/learning/baby-facts/peek.html
3. Daily Christian Quote. (2011). *I lift my eyes.* Retrieved January 10, 2011, from http://dailychristianquote.com/dcqintimacy3.html

Taking the Highway:

1. Vos, H.F. (1999). *Nelson's new illustrated Bible manners & customs: How the people of the Bible really lived* (p. 433). Nashville: Thomas Nelson Inc.
2. *Dictionary.com.* (2011). Retrieved February 2, 2011, from http://dictionary.reference.com/browse/excellence
3. *Ochristian.com.* (n.d.). Retrieved February 2, 2011, from http://christian-quotes.ochristian.com/John-R.-Rice-Quotes/

Something Beautiful:

1. *Greek Bible.* (2001-2010). Retrieved December 22, 2010, from http://www.greekbible.com/1.php?a)/gw_v-3pai-s--_p
2. Daily Christian Quote. (2011). *I Lift My Eyes.* Retrieved January 5, 2011, from http://dailychristianquote.com/dcqpatience-waiting.html

Letter Shredder:

1. *Dictionary.com.* (2011). Retrieved February 9, 2011, from http://dictionary.reference.com/browse/inferiority
2. *Dictionary.com.* (2011). Retrieved February 9, 2011, from http://dictionary.reference.com/browse/insecurity

3. *The Online Greek Bible*. (2001-2010). Retrieved January 2, 2011, from http://www.greekbible.com/1.php?u(pernika/w_v-1pai-p--_p

4. Mounce, D.W. (2003). *Basics of Biblical Greek grammar*. Great Rapids, MI: Zondervan.

5. *The Online Greek Bible*. (2001-2010). Retrieved January 9, 2011, from http://www.greekbible.com/1.php?suntri/bw_v-3fai-s--_p

6. *Think Exist*. (1999-2010). Retrieved January 10, 2011, from http://www.thinkexist.com/quotes/with/keyword/satan/

Rock Solid Arms:

1. In Depth Info. (1999-2011). *W.J. Rayment*. Retrieved February 2, 2011, from http://www.indepthinfo.com/articles/anchors.shtml

2. *Christian Quotes*. (2002-2010). Retrieved February 9, 2011, from http://christianquotes.org/author/quotes/12/40

The Sweetest Words:

1. *Tentmaker*. (2010). Retrieved January 11, 2011, from http://www.tentmaker.org/Quotes/repentancequotes.htm

The Phenomenal Exchange:

1. *Christiangay.com*. (n.d.). Retrieved February 11, 2011, from http://www.christiangay.com/he_loves/false.htm

2. Names of God. (n.d.). Retrieved February 23, 2011. from http://www.clarion-call.org/extras/names.htm

3. *Famous Quotes*. (n.d.). Retrieved February 26, 2011, from http://www.brainyquote.com/quotes/authors/j/jean_paul.html

Weapons of Wisdom:

1. Vos, H.F. (1999). *Nelson's new illustrated Bible manners & customs: How the people of the Bible really lived* (p. 167). Nashville: Thomas Nelson Inc.
2. *Famous Quotes.* (n.d.). Retrieved February 9, 2011, from http://www.brainyquote.com/quotes/keywords/wise.html

The Hundred and Sixty Minutes:

1. Davis, J.K. (2009). *Rapunzel stories in modern literature: Contemporary versions of the children's classic fairy tale.* Retrieved (date), from http://www.suite101.com/content/rapunzel-stories-in-modern-literature-a158616
2. *Grimm Stories.* (n.d.). Retrieved January 31, 2011, from http://www.grimmstories.com/en/grimm_fairy-tales/rapunzel
3. *Ochristian.com.* (1999-2010). Retrieved February 26, 2011, from http://christian-quotes.ochristian.com/christian-quotes_ochristian.cgi?query=trust&action=Search

One Suave God:

1. Chapman, L. (2011). Jehovah-Shammah, the Lord is present. *Minerva Web Works LLC.* Retrieved January 20, 2011, from http://www.bellaonline.com/articles/art64717.asp
2. John, D.C. (1995). *The nations of the bible: Amalekites.* Retrieved January 15, 2011, from http://www.isaiah58.com/broadcasters/amel.htm
3. *Famous Quotes.* (n.d.). Retrieved January 10, 2011, from http://www.brainyquote.com/quotes/keywords/faithful.html

Without Boarders:

1. Dowley, T., John, H., Robert, D., & David, F. (Eds). (2002). *Introduction to the history of Christianity* (pp. 440). Minneapolis: Augsburg Books.
2. Dowley, T., John, H., Robert, D., & David, F. (Eds). (2002). *Introduction to the history of Christianity* (pp. 441-444). Minneapolis: Augsburg Books.
3. Dowley, T., John, H., Robert, D., & David, F. (Eds). (2002). *Introduction to the history of Christianity* (p. 66). Minneapolis: Augsburg Books.
4. Silent World Ministries International. (n.d.). Retrieved February 26, 2011, from http://www.silentwordministries.org/index.php?option=com_content&view=article&id=393:missquotes&catid=43:ideas-for-missions-conferences&Itemid=63

Unstoppable Romance:

1. Dowley, T., John, H., Robert, D., & David, F. (Eds). (2002). *Introduction to the history of Christianity* (pp. 440). Minneapolis: Augsburg Books.
2. *In Christ Ministries India.* (2010). Retrieved February 10, 2011, from http://icmi.co.za/ermi/

Divine Persistence:

1. Cauchi, T. (2009). Revival library. *Prayer.* Retrieved February 2, 2011, from http://www.revival-library.org/leadership/rq_prayer.php

Fruit Bearer:

1. Dowley, T., John, H., Robert, D., & David, F. (Eds). (2002). *Introduction to the history of Christianity* (p. 80). Minneapolis: Augsburg Books.

2. Encyclopaedia Britannica. (2011). *Charles Martel.* Retrieved January 12, 2011, from http://www.britannica.com/EBchecked/topic/107383/Charl es-Martel
3. Onthewing.org. (1988). Retrieved (2011), from http://www.onthewing.org/user/CH05%20-%20Missions.pdf
4. Quote Garden. (2010). *Quotations about helping and making a difference.* Retrieved January 10, 2011, from http://www.quotegarden.com/helping.html

The *"Even If"* Attitude:

1. Bethge, Eberhard. (2000). *Dietrich Bonhoeffer*: A biography (p. 927). Minneapolis: Augsburg Fortress.
2. *Think Exist.* (1999-2010). Retrieved January 22, 2011, from http://thinkexist.com/quotes/corrie-ten-boom/

Approved at the Gate:

1. Dictionary.com. (2011). Retrieved February 9, 2011, from http://dictionary.reference.com/browse/citizen
2. The Titi Tudorancea Bulletin. (2010, September). *Citizenship.* Retrieved February 2, 2011, from http://www.tititudorancea.com/z/citizenship.htm
3. Ehow. (1999-2011). *How to join the army as a non-U.S. citizen.* Retrieved February 2, 2011, from http://www.ehow.com/how_2248012_join-army-as-nonus-citizen.html
4. *Wholesome Words.* (2011). Retrieved February 9, 2011, from http://www.wholesomewords.org/echoes/taylor.html

The Radical Recollection:

1. Dowley, T., John, H., Robert, D., & David, F. (Eds). (2002). *Introduction to the history of Christianity* (p. 29). Minneapolis: Augsburg Books.
2. *Finest Quotes*. (n.d.). Retrieved February 9, 2011, from http://www.finestquotes.com/quote_with-keyword-Compassion-page-7.htm

About Author

Janell Ward's first published devotional, "He Said it All" was released in 2005. Her love for the written word pushed her pursuit and completion of a B.S. degree in English with the concentration of Creative Writing. With a strong love for theology she completed advanced Greek courses along with several religion classes.

Having traveled to over ten countries throughout Europe and South America, on mission trips and school projects, Janell has had numerous experiences with sharing the gospel internationally. People who know Janell refer to her as being courageous, compassionate, and zealous in prayer. Janell claims her future goals are, "simple... I just want to change lives through teaching, traveling, and writing."

Beyond all her hopes in life, Janell states, "I live to understand the meaning of 'I am my beloved and my beloved is mine.'" With a warm smile she continues, "My life is all for my King. He is fanatic about loving me. I should be fanatic about loving him."

You may contact Janell Ward at

Janellrward@hotmail.com